BLINDED BY THE
LIES

BLINDED BY THE
LIES

DALE & SANDY LARSEN

While this book is intended for the reader's personal enjoyment and profit, it is also intended for group study. A Leader's Guide with Victor Multiuse Transparency Masters is available from your local bookstore or from the publisher.

VICTOR BOOKS®

A DIVISION OF SCRIPTURE PRESS PUBLICATIONS INC.
USA CANADA ENGLAND

Unless otherwise noted, Scripture quotations are from the *Holy Bible, New International Version,* © 1973, 1978, 1984, International Bible Society. Used by permission of Zondervan Bible Publishers. Quotations marked KJV are taken from *Authorized* (King James) *Version.* Quotations marked PH are taken from J.B. Phillips: *The New Testament in Modern English,* Revised Edition, © J.B. Phillips, 1958, 1960, 1972, permission of Macmillan Publishing Co. and Collins Publishers.

Recommended Dewey Decimal Classification: PERSONAL RELIGION: CONDUCT OF CHRISTIAN LIFE
Suggested Subject Heading: 248.4

Library of Congress Catalog Card Number: 89-060164
ISBN: 0-89693-680-5

TABLE OF CONTENTS

For the
Cut-and-Run
Players

PREFACE

Welcome to the Age of Information, where we're continually torpedoed by messages telling us what we should do, be, eat, drink, wear, own, and think. We didn't ask for the advice, but we're getting it anyway through ads, music, movies, TV shows, management and education seminars, and what can only be described as the atmosphere we breathe in, simply by living here and now.

Skillfully composed and slickly packaged, the stories and images enter through our eyes and ears and become lodged in our minds as part of our everyday assumptions about life.

We know we shouldn't copy the violent and/or immoral lifestyles we see on the screen. We also know we can't believe everything advertisements tell us; they're intended to make us buy things whether we need them or not. Yet even if we don't rush out and buy the latest electronic miracle, our expectations of what we "must have" increase a bit. And even though we don't indulge in the sins of the stars, we may become more tolerant of sin because it is presented to us as normal life.

In this book we desire to examine the subtle lies which are taking hold in our culture, compare them to Scripture, and suggest a positive, Christian response.

God's Word is more powerful than all the false messages which try to blind us with their glitter. If we keep exposing ourselves to its truth, the Bible will become an intimate part of us and crowd out the falsehoods we see and hear.

Armed with the "full armor of God" (Eph. 6:11), we can keep from believing the lies and we can help people who are still blinded by them. We can show mercy, leavened with wisdom, and be true helpers to all people who are looking for truth in all the wrong places.

MESSAGE ONE:

You Can Have It All. You Deserve It!

"Garage-saling" is a major sport in our area. A trip through the weekly garage sale circuit reveals piles of yesterday's gadgets that people just "had to have": personal hot dog cookers, mini deep fryers, and last year's outlandish fashions—now priced at only a few dollars or less. People bought those things at their original prices because they were told a certain possession would make them happy, or a unique piece of clothing would make them look just right, or a new gadget would make them more efficient. Garage sales are full of material evidence that people have bought into false promises and were disappointed.

Hurrying from garage sale to garage sale, we tell each other "I'm so busy lately!" How did we come to accept the message that we have to do everything and be everything to everybody?

God offers us a balanced life in which we will have some things and go without others. We will be able to do some things but forced to forego others according to His will. We find fulfillment at the pace and place He has for us.

CHAPTER ONE

Happiness Is Just a Possession Away

The engagement was broken, but the young man's mother showed me pictures of the apartment her son and his fiancée had planned to share. I expected to see sparsely furnished rooms, perhaps some older furniture inherited from Mom and Dad. Instead, I stared in amazement at photos that looked like something out of *House Beautiful.* Room after room was filled with brass lamps, great, puffy earthtone furniture, oriental rugs, custom wallpaper adorned with contemporary paintings.... *This* showcase was to have been the newlyweds' first apartment? Their parents should be doing so well!

What drive had forced these young people to accumulate all those photogenic, upscale furnishings (and a large debt) so early in the life of their relationship—a relationship that was rocky anyway?

What caused them to act this way is actually no mystery. All of us experience the same drive in some form or other. It talks to us from all corners of our culture. Sometimes it whispers; sometimes it shouts. It comes from advertising and our peers and our own self-centered nature: You don't have to wait for anything you want. You can have everything now. In fact, you should have everything now. You deserve it!

The message "You can have it all now" comes in various forms: "You can have it all materially, professionally, sexually, financially, physically, even spiritually!"

Well, who wouldn't be enticed by such an attractive message? Who wouldn't prefer to have what he wants now, instead of having to be patient? Who likes to wait for anything?

Needy People

The message "You can have it all" thrives on our natural feeling of need. If we went through this world naturally satisfied, we wouldn't feel a desire to "have it all"—we wouldn't feel a need for anything beyond what we have. But we are needy. And we know it. Hunger, loneliness, discomfort, longing for purpose—all drive us to search for something—anything—which promises to fill us up physically and emotionally.

God created us to be needy. He made us to be hungry for Himself. But our hungers, distorted by sin, often don't differentiate between the real meat and the junk food. What our spirits feel as a hunger for God, our hearts and bodies often misinterpret as a desire for all kinds of other things.

Our own contemporary culture is a vivid example of a populace madly misreading its own spiritual hunger as the desire for more and better material comforts.

The mistaken identity is easy to understand. Material comforts feel good. They surround us with ease when life knocks us around. They soothe and distract us from troubles. They even introduce us to the world as valuable people, for surely we must have something on the ball if we can afford so many nice possessions, and certainly we must be good people if we own good things.

Burdened by Our Things

A few years ago Sandy wrote a book for teens entitled *Things*. It spoke up for a biblical perspective on material possessions: enjoy them and use them as on loan from God but don't make them into gods or let them control your life.

That summer it was easy for her to write with a detachment toward material things; we were living out of our car, camping while we decided on a different place to live. It was enjoyable to be unencumbered (by choice) by possessions. The little we had with us that summer was enough.

That was six years ago. Since then, we have acquired a house with seven rooms plus a storage area, and most of those spaces are filled. Sandy confesses to mixed feelings about these treasures. Every few months she takes a tour through the house and relentlessly throws or gives things away. But there's always another garage sale or trip to K-Mart coming up, and the spaces always get filled up again.

This houseful of stuff doesn't represent any great expenditure of money. Because we both love well-worn collectibles, most of our things are other people's throwaways which we have reconstituted. But even unique secondhand stuff threatens to become a burden. What happens when we move again? How important will this baggage *really* turn out to be to us if we are called on to get rid of it? Or if (as happened to friends of ours) we had a fire? Do we actually believe and live the truths in the book, *Things?* Or are we fooling ourselves?

The End of Greed?

We're not alone in our questioning of the value which should be placed on lavish amounts of material goods. The

'80s were dubbed "The Decade of Greed," and in its first issue of 1988, a news magazine was already declaring the decade dead of exhaustion.

Today there are signs that some yuppies are finding volunteer work a better means of self-fulfillment than chasing material prosperity: "There are signs of increased altruism in the '90s as well. Forty-nine percent of respondents to a Newsweek poll say they are involved in charity or social-service activity, up from 36 percent in 1986" (Karen Springen and Jennifer Foote, "The Eighties Are Over," *Newsweek*, January 4, 1988, p. 48).

We hope the article is correct about a new U.S. trend for the '90s. Yet no matter what the decade, greed is never completely out of style. The nagging feeling that one more thing will bring satisfaction is always with us.

When we think of the "toys" we still consider necessary, we are a long way from the satisfaction Paul spoke of in Philippians 4:12: "I know what it is to be in need, and I know what it is to have plenty. I have learned the secret of being content in any and every situation, whether well fed or hungry, whether living in plenty or in want."

When we begin to take the Creator for granted and fill our lives only with the things He has provided—disregarding the Giver—then we have certainly lost our way. And if our lives become filled with the acquisition and enjoyment of our possessions, we have bowed to worship another god: the god of our own pleasure. In and of themselves things are not bad, but they always have the potential to become the possessers instead of the possessed.

Benefits of Possessions
Everything we own is on the way to the dump, and some things will get there even sooner than the fine print on their guarantees promises.

Then what benefit is there in owning material goods? A great deal.

● Material goods can make us grateful to God, who lends them to us.

● They can teach us responsibility as we respect and care for His creation.

● They can teach us that what we have is not really ours but His.

● They can make our lives easier and more convenient.

● They give us a tangible means of expressing our creativity.

● They can satisfy our physical senses as we use them and look at them and enjoy them.

● And as they break and rust and wear out, material things can graphically remind us that this world is passing away and that nothing here is permanent except our souls.

We mentioned our friends who had a fire. It centered in the basement and destroyed a workshop full of tools. Insurance promptly paid for everything, and our friend went to the hardware to replace the tools. But hard as it is to believe, he reported that it actually wasn't much fun walking in and plunking down $1,000 of insurance money at the hardware store. The new tools just didn't seem to have the same value. The old ones had each been carefully considered and bought on the basis of how much they'd be used and whether they were really affordable right then. They had intrinsic value beyond their original price tags because of the care put into each purchase. The new ones—well, they just came in one bundle, utilitarian but without emotion. But still he bought the new tools.

Holding Possessions Lightly
Paul was enjoying no placid lake or campfire when he wrote the letter to the Philippians. Quite the opposite: he

was in prison for preaching Christ (1:13); in chains (1:7, 13-14, 17); uncertain about his own life, thinking this imprisonment might even lead to his death (1:20, 2:17); concerned about insincere rival preachers filling the vacuum while he was out of circulation (1:15-17); troubled by disagreements within the church he began (4:2); and unsupported by the other churches (4:15). Paul's situation was hardly a comfortable picture of success. He could easily have felt deprived of the comforts of material wealth and professional achievement.

Yet, Christians over the centuries have repeatedly turned to Paul's letter to the Philippians as a source of joy. In the worst of circumstances, Paul was glad for what he had.

And what did he have? Not material things, certainly. The letter was written to thank the Philippians for sending a material gift, but even in his thank-you, Paul made it clear that the gift was not what counted (4:11, 17).

Paul possessed the greatest possession of all, which is not material and which will outlast all things material. He had "Him who gives me strength" (4:13)—that is, Christ.

Paul did not lift up poverty and deprivation in some sort of exalted spiritual position. Most of us would agree with the person who reported, "I've been rich and I've been poor, and believe me, rich is better." Sure it's pleasant to have things. Paul meant that we can and should find contentment in poverty if it's our lot, but he does not say that abundance will destroy our contentment.

The secret is not how much or how little we have but how lightly we hold on to our possessions. If we're grateful for the things and use them well—and if they can then burn up and we still find peace in knowing we have Christ with us—then we have an attitude toward material things which is close to the biblical attitude Paul promotes.

We know a family who is blessed with material wealth.

To be around these people, you'd never know they had money to burn. They look, dress, and sound ordinary. Nothing in their lives is flashy. Their money has gone toward supporting numerous missionaries and fixing up an old lodge where Christian groups as well as the members of their own large extended family can come for retreats. Until recently they owned a large house in which various students and other needy people lived with them; they also owned several smaller houses for the use of people such as missionaries on furlough. They *enjoy* the motorboats and the water skis and the enormous stone fireplace; yet, being around them, we have the strong sense that they are not very tightly attached to any of these things. In fact, they recently gave up the big house and now live in one far more humble than their means might dictate. That's all right with them.

Here is a family wisely using the wealth God has given them—not for themselves but for Him and for other people.

God's Offer

Well, fine, you might say, but I don't own several houses, and I don't have room to take in homeless people or money to support myriads of missionaries.

But we do all have things—things which we can use for the Lord or for our own indulgence.

We live in a time of more laborsaving and timesaving devices than ever before. Yet when any church attempts a new program, people just can't find the time to help out.

What are we doing with the time technology saves us? Are we spending our newly freed-up time just entertaining ourselves?

"Just one more possession" is an attractive trap. "Whoever loves money never has money enough; whoever loves wealth is never satisfied with his income" (Ecc. 5:10). Once our hearts are set on things instead of on Christ, it's a guarantee that things will never satisfy; they'll only make us hungrier for more things.

"You can have it all"? Never. Because once we think we "have it all" materially, we will still want more.

Physical things are a small part of what God offers us. They aren't the ultimate or even the largest part of what He has for us. He offers in addition to the things, and sometimes even instead of the things, a relationship with Himself. His imprisoned servant Paul wrote, "I consider everything a loss compared to the surpassing greatness of knowing Christ Jesus my Lord, for whose sake I have lost all things" (Phil. 3:8). Remarkable words in the 1980s, but living words for the 1990s and beyond.

CHAPTER TWO

Image Is What Matters

You can almost feel the brush snapping and slashing as you break trail through the clothing catalog that came in the mail today. On every page, a collection of craggy men brave the elements in their rugged garments. These must be the clothes in which to head out and live off the land.

Except—there's a smooth edge of glamor in the way the models stand gazing into the forested mountains. Every hair is in place—or meticulously out of place—and there's not a trace of mud, sweat, or grass stains on their impeccably rugged clothing.

Now we gaze at the price tags of those clothes and laugh and throw the catalog away. Here in the north woods, where rustic living is a reality, no outdoorsman would risk such costly duds on a thorny expedition in the real world, and nobody actually living in "back-to-nature" style could afford them!

Now why would a guy whose experience with nature is limited to his backyard want to look like he's about to set off to find the Northwest Passage or hunt elephants? Is he fooling anyone? Of course not. These clothes are made to project the aura, the romantic illusion—the image—he desires other people to have of him: that despite his urban office job, at heart he's actually a blood-and-nerve explorer-type, longing for the real world at the remote reaches of the wilderness. If only he'd been born a hundred years ago when men tested their mettle by slashing through the jungles or struggling to the Pole.

Maybe he's actually that type and maybe he isn't. What matters is that's how he wants people to *think* of him, so he spends money on this kind of clothing.

The urban wearer of the explorer look has a lot of company. Most of us fret about what people think of us. No one is immune to the nagging question, "How am I coming across?"

An Image Campaign
The presidential campaign of 1988 was a vivid illustration of this concern over image. The content of the news from this campaign—The Battle of Images—was astonishing. We heard surprisingly little about any candidate's philosophy, beliefs, or practical plans for leading the United States into the 1990s. What we did hear about, endlessly, was the latest bend and turn in each candidate's evolving image. What each man was *trying to seem to be* made more news than who he actually is. It was as though we were being asked to judge a person's character by looking at a series of posed portraits of him in a photo album without ever meeting the real person.

Since modern presidential campaigns are carried out via TV's quick glimpses and snatches of sound, image inevitably carries a lot of weight. We have to acknowledge the phenomenon, and it should receive critical analysis as a factor in politics. But in the 1988 campaign image itself became the substance of the campaign.

The voice, the frown wrinkles, the posture, the mannerisms—what do any of these externals have to do with what each man believes or how he would govern? You'd think we were electing not a person but a hologram! A would-be presidential candidate who cannot meet the physical requirements of looking like a presidential candidate is out of luck.

Stephen Hawking is one of the world's greatest physicists. A victim of Lou Gehrig's disease, Hawking is paralyzed and cannot speak. He gets around on a motorized wheelchair and communicates by computer, using one-finger commands to construct sentences which are then spoken by computerized voice. Could Stephen Hawking (disregarding the fact that he is British) ever be elected President of the U.S.? He hardly looks like a presidential candidate. For that matter, he doesn't look like what he actually is. No one would cast him for the brilliant scientist role in a science fiction movie. How obvious in Hawking's case that external image tells us nothing about the inner workings of the person.

The Image Smorgasbord
As long as we don't go to extremes, is there anything wrong with choosing to project a certain image to the people around us? After all, we all have to look and act like *something*, and most of us would like some control over how we come across to others.

These days, an infinite number of images are available for us to put on. The carpenter used to be the carpenter, and the nobleman used to be the nobleman, but those days are gone. Now we can look and act like anybody we want to, and we can change our image at will. Preppie, yuppie, adventurer, jock, technocrat, artist, back-to-nature buff, fitness addict, cowboy, achiever, acquirer—the possibilities go on and on.

From this smorgasbord of externals, it's assumed that we will select an image which will advance our own purposes. Business people are even hiring image consultants to reconstruct how they're coming across—how they dress, talk, walk, behave—so their external appearance will help them influence their associates to the maximum. We are urged to put on an image, not because it accurately expresses us, but because it gets us what we want.

California builder Lance Mortensen specializes in creating dream houses which are furnished to the last detail.

> These are dream houses for people too busy to dream. . . . The houses are not merely furnished, they are set up and running with all life-support systems in place: utilities, pool heater, cable television. . . . It is not just convenience Mortensen has to offer, it is security, the security that comes from knowing that the myriad inanimate objects that surround them—from the Lenox china to the Magnalilte saucepans to the Braun coffee makers—are unmistakably appropriate to their place and station in the world. "People don't trust their own taste," says Mortensen. (Jerry Adler with Pamela Abramson, "For Sale: The Rich Look," *Newsweek*, June 22, 1987, p. 80).

It is ironic that we look to others to tell us how we should express our true selves. Writer Michael Solomon explains, "Most of us spend a lot of money decorating our homes. Since we express our identities through our surroundings, we tend to be emotionally involved in these purchases. But, ironically, for many people this self-expression may be packaged by strangers." The decorating by strangers extends to personal dress as well as draperies. "As the president of one wardrobe consulting firm bluntly advised professional readers in the *Philadelphia Inquirer*, 'You are a product yourself. People view you like a package of cheese' " ("Counselors of Taste," *Psychology Today*, January 1988, pp. 52–53).

Few of us can hire image consultants to tell us how we ought to look. But it's easy to regularly accept as normal and desirable the looks invented for us by others, whether or not they accurately express our own personalities. And since few of us measure up to the perfection of the images we see, we wind up frustrated, feeling we fall short of the mark defined for us.

When our next-door neighbor was pregnant, she looked better than most people look when they're *not* pregnant. After Todd Jr. was born, Diane still looked great. Sandy went over to visit her and found a copy of a high-tech fitness magazine on the coffee table. The pages glistened with models in bright leotards covering "perfect" bodies. "Doesn't that magazine make you sick?" Diane asked. "If only I could look like that!" Instead of looking in the mirror at how good she actually looked, she was looking in a magazine and discovering how bad she looked.

Many of us find that the latest swimsuit only exposes our lumpiness instead of making us look like we stepped out of *Sports Illustrated*. The comparisons go on and on. Is the grass on our front lawns thin and brittle instead of luxuriant? Do our teenaged children not want to play tennis with us every evening nor excel at the cello? Is our dream car going the way of all machinery, and we are ashamed to drive it into the church parking lot?

Where is the real person under the externals we display to the world? When image is elevated to all-important, there's a devaluing of the true person who doesn't dare to come out from behind the mask. And beneath the image we may forget who we really are, if we ever knew.

A Really Good Christian

What does a really good Christian look like? "Like anyone," you answer. But search further in your mind, and you'll find a picture of what a "really good Christian" should be. The dimensions and demeanor of this "really good Christian" vary from age to age and church to church. Often we get our image from a particular Christian who influenced us strongly, perhaps the one who first showed Christ to us by his or her life. That particular way of living then became for us *the* Christian lifestyle, and that person became *the* ideal Christian.

Perhaps our ideal person is very knowledgeable and wise with immense portions of the Bible committed to memory, unstumpable in discussions of theology and church history.

Or perhaps this person is never down, going through life with a bubbly, positive attitude.

Does a really good Christian live very simply and give away all excess goods and money to the Lord's work?

Or does this person dress for success and follow the upward track financially as well as spiritually, demonstrating the Lord's tangible blessings?

Does he raise his hands in worship? Does she kneel to pray in church? Do they look clean-cut, exuberant, and physically fit? Do they dress conservatively and modestly? Do they have a large family in order to raise up many souls for God?

What kind of car does this true Christian drive? A nice (but not flashy) car to present a good appearance to the world? Or an old beater because all excess money has been given to world missions?

Would he be caught dead drinking a wine cooler? Does she wear makeup? If so, how much?

We could go on and on, but of course the truth is that none of the above tests tell us whether a person is a "really good Christian." Yet consciously or subconsciously, we all answer the question "What does a really good Christian look like?" with our own various mental images.

Many disputes in the church happen precisely because people differ on their private impressions of what a true Christian looks like or does. We sound each other's spiritual depth by our preconceived ideals of how a real Christian ought to act or appear. The trouble is, we often don't communicate those mental images to each other (largely because we don't know we have them). All we know is the other person rubs us the wrong way and isn't acting like he ought to if he's a good Christian. Maybe he'll mature, but until then he can't be trusted.

Idolizing Our Leaders
Sometimes we take the opposite approach. We idolize a glamorous singer or preacher who always *looks* so radiantly spiritual on stage. *Surely that Christian has it all together* we think—just look at that smile, note that confident attitude, hear those words of praise to the Lord.

One fan of a popular female Christian singer bristled when the singer was criticized for a particular business decision she had made. "She must have been led of the Lord to do what she did," he said, "because I just know she follows the Lord in everything she does."

We hope he's right, but how does *he* know? How can he, who has only seen this person from afar, possibly know what her motives are? Give us a month to live in that person's home, travel the concert circuit with her, watch her when the sound equipment isn't working right, or talk with her when she comes offstage after the show and then we can tell you something of what's in her heart.

Fairly or unfairly, many Christians who are looked up to for leadership today are known and followed from a comfortable distance, through electronics or from a box seat. Most of us have little idea what these heroes are really like.

If we're honest about it, how many of us want our lives intimately scrutinized by other believers? It's safer to stay behind the image of spirituality.

Jesus: The Authentic Image of God

In contrast to the images we create for ourselves and the images we project on others, stands the life of Jesus, representing the amazing truth that "the Word became flesh and lived for a while among us" (John 1:14). Once we see God's willingness to reveal Himself to us and to be known by us, He puts to shame all our self-disguising and image-projecting.

Unseen, unheard, God could have remained unknown by His creation. But He did the opposite. God came into this world as Christ, a human being, one of us—seeable, touchable, knowable.

As remarkable as it is that God lived with us, perhaps it is even more remarkable that God let us live with Him and in such intimacy. Jesus' disciple and close friend, John wrote about "that which was from the beginning, which we have heard, which we have seen with our eyes, which we have looked at and our hands have touched" (1 John 1:1). God let us know Him under trying circumstances, catch Him when He was vulnerable, hurt Him, even watch Him die.

The Gospels present an image of Christ which (unlike the phony posing we so easily adopt) is an *authentic* image. A crowd of Jesus' screaming fans did not write the books we have about His life. These are no celebrity biographies full of glitz and glamour. The New Testament is the written witness of those who knew and lived with Jesus and their close associates. They give us no hyped-up image of the Son of God; they show Him as they knew Him, day in and day out. We see Jesus doing miracles and addressing great crowds, and we also see Him tired, hungry, thirsty, angry, praying in desperation, grieving over a dead friend, and suffering physically and mentally.

When we see this true image of Jesus, we literally see the image of God, for "anyone who has seen me has seen the Father" (John 14:9).

One of Christ's early opponents prided himself on knowing God's Word and God's will. He initially thought that the man Jesus had nothing to do with God. Then Paul met the real Jesus and was changed forever. He gave up his worldly view of Christ and began regarding Him as the Son of God (2 Cor. 5:16). Paul later referred to Christ as "the image of the invisible God, the firstborn over all creation" (Col. 1:15).

The Greek word Paul used for image here is *eikon*, which carries both the meanings of "representation" and "manifestation" of God. Christ was no shell of a man putting on niceties to make people accept Him. He acted with all the goodness of God because He was genuinely and fully God here on this earth. "For God was pleased to have all His fullness dwell in Him, and through Him to reconcile to Himself all things, whether things on earth or things in heaven, by making peace through His blood, shed on the cross" (Col. 1:19-20).

The book of Hebrews begins with praise for Christ the Son as "the radiance of God's glory and the exact representation ["express image" in KJV] of His being, sustaining all things by His powerful word" (Heb. 1:3). Here the word translated "image" or "representation" is *charakter*, which originally meant an engraving tool or the impression of a stamp or die. Christ showed the very character of God because He was wholly God, not simply on the outside but through and through.

Conforming to His Image

Christ was thoroughly genuine in all His compassion, joy, wisdom, peace, and forgiveness. As His followers, we often lack such genuineness in our character, but the hope He always holds out to us is that His Spirit will transform us from within, working to make us as genuine as our Lord. "And if the Spirit of Him who raised Jesus from the dead is living in you, He who raised Christ from the dead will also give life to your mortal bodies through His Spirit, who lives in you" (Rom. 8:11).

Later in the same letter, Paul urged the Romans, "in view of God's mercy, to offer your bodies as living sacrifices, holy and pleasing to God—which is your spiritual worship. Do not conform any longer to the pattern of this world, but be transformed by the renewing of your mind. Then you will be able to test and approve what God's will is—His good, pleasing and perfect will" (Rom. 12:1-2).

When we find the qualities of Christ lacking in our lives, we tend to attack the problem—from the outside in. We all like people to *think* they see Christlike qualities in us, so we try to make ourselves *seem to* possess those qualities. We smile in church; we tell a person who offends us, "That's okay, it didn't bother me," as we grit our teeth. We smooth the worry wrinkles on our faces before we go in the church door. We carefully conceal our sins and struggles from each other, oblivious to the fact that Christ, whom we call our Lord, willingly revealed Himself.

We may defend our secretive behavior by saying that Jesus had nothing to be ashamed of while we have plenty of things within us that would cause us shame if other people knew. The truth and the irony is that the "other people" know their own hearts all too well and know they aren't perfect either. And they may even be busy hiding themselves from us! If only we could all be brave enough to reveal ourselves to each other—not so that we can gloat over each other's faults but so that we can support each other and bring each other to God in prayer.

Like any good counsel, self-revelation can be taken to a dangerous extreme. There are times it's not appropriate to let out all our anger on the nearest victim. And some private concerns should not be shared with a whole churchful of people or even an entire Bible-study group. Not every sin needs to be confessed to every ready ear, or every interpersonal conflict made public.

For example, if another Christian has done us wrong, God's Word tells us to "go and show him his fault, just between the two of you.... But if he will not listen, take one or two others along.... If he refuses to listen to them, tell it to the church" (Matt. 18:15-17).

Most of us err the other way; we hide too much from each other because we're so painfully conscious of our image. Time and energy are wasted trying to seem like Christ instead of letting Christ be Himself in us.

Let's go back to the antiseptic bushwhacker clothes in that catalog we threw away at the start of this chapter. The message is clear: men, this is the image that will make you acceptable. And perhaps it will help you fit in, in some circles, temporarily, until fashions change. But God sees the inner person regardless of the external trappings. God told Samuel, when Samuel was sure that David's big brother Eliab would become the chosen king of Israel to succeed Saul: "The Lord does not look at the things man looks at. Man looks at the outward appearance, but the Lord looks at the heart" (1 Sam. 16:7).

We are not necessarily called to go around in dowdy, outdated clothes. There's nothing intrinsically holy about wearing fashions from ten years ago as opposed to this season's latest. Trying hard to look *not* with-it can be as big a trap as scrambling to have the latest. Christ's approach is from a wholly different direction: to renew us from within and bring us to a place where the externals cease to matter, or at least to matter so much.

As long as our aim is to adopt the right appearance (whether successful, rugged, sensual, or even righteous), we make the image of Christ secondary. And we mask or even lose the unique person He has made us to be.

Instead of all our scrambling after image, we need to have the courage to be our honest selves from the inside out, as God made us to be.

CHAPTER THREE

You Can Do It All— and You Should

Remember in the first chapter we said that Sandy periodically goes through the house throwing things away then accumulates more fascinating, unique objects? She also does that with her schedule. Every few months she says, "I'm doing too much" and cuts out several activities. And of course that leaves holes in her schedule, which she can now fill with more activities.

"Blessed are those who go around in circles," we used to say when we were in junior high, "for they shall be known as big wheels."

Recently at the library, two experts on local history showed photographs from a hundred years ago. Then as now, winter here was bitter, the growing season was short, and farmland had to be carved from the woods. It was an isolated rough-hewn area of mining, logging, and commercial fishing. We imagine those early pioneers working constantly just to stay alive.

The surprise is that the people in the pictures are all *relaxing*. They're picnicking on island parks, riding excursion boats on Lake Superior, or socializing in front of stores and churches. They stare out from group poses of baseball teams by the dozen, brass bands, garden clubs, and marching units. There's even—no kidding—the "World's Largest All-Girl Ukulele Chorus." There must be fifty girls in that picture. Sandy couldn't get that many kids in Sunday School if she gave away five-pound boxes of chocolates.

These pictures leave us with a stumping question: Where did people find the time for all that recreation back then? Some of us can barely find a few minutes to run to the convenience store to rent a movie for the VCR. Wisconsin residents of a century ago who had to find time to chop enough wood to stay warm at thirty degrees below zero, grow food and put it up for winter, pump their own water, milk their own cows, and butcher their own chickens still found leisure time to make their own entertainment.

Our lives today, loaded with time-saving conveniences, seem more compulsively frantic than theirs.

The Frantic Rat Race

Much of the compulsion we feel comes from what our culture tells us we're supposed to be doing with our lives.

Elizabeth M. Whelan, a successful science and health writer, tells how she assumed without doubt that there were four life goals she could and should achieve in the twenty years after high school:

A good education. An intelligent, career-oriented husband. A child (maybe two or three). A beautiful suburban home, just like the one my parents had. By my mid-30s ... I expected to be a happily-married, college-educated mother living in a charming house and, I hoped, with enough outside interests to be a contributing member of my community. Now, at age 36, not only have I met these expectations, but I am playing so many different roles that even my highly elastic nerves have been stretched to the snapping point" ("Confessions of a 'Superwoman,'" *Across the Board*, December 1980, p. 17).

Ironically, many of our northern Wisconsin neighbors moved here to *escape* that rat race, and they've found it waiting for them here in the woods. One writer/photographer/nurse told us, "We moved up here from the Twin Cities so life wouldn't be so hectic, and life is more hectic than ever." He has a young family and is working two jobs, publishing his own monthly newspaper, and building a house.

We know another couple who moved here from New York State to get into self-sufficient living. They had had enough of fast-paced Eastern life. They got night jobs in town to support themselves while they started their back-to-nature adventure. They explained, "Our idea was we'd both work full-time, but the jobs weren't going to be our main thing." Reality proved they couldn't do what they expected to do. By the time they made the twice-daily twenty-five-mile commute on dusty or icy roads, then tried to work at building their log home, they were as frazzled as they had been in the urban climb back East. By the third time they failed at digging a well and found out electric hookup to their remote home would cost several thousand dollars, their attempts at self-sufficiency collapsed—and, tragically, so did their marriage.

We can move away from the busy city, but we can't move away from the busyness within ourselves. Franticness on the inside spells frazzledness on the outside, whether it's up in a high-rise or down on the farm.

Mind-boggling Amounts of Choices

The rat race is within us. But it's also encouraged by the external messages our culture feeds us through advertising, TV and film story lines, even our education. We're up against something the All-Girl Ukulele Chorus never had to think about: a mind-boggling spread of choices of what we will do with ourselves. Life (we're told) is a smorgasbord of possibilities; we can and should have whatever we want and do and be whatever we like. We're pushing a bottomless cart down aisles of opportunity (we're told), and we should fulfill ourselves by indulging in any and all pursuits we like.

The uke-playing, young Wisconsin ladies didn't have to worry about a lot of choices. Music was probably their main cultural and social outlet; the rest of their time was spent working at home. That's why the chorus got such a huge turnout. If there aren't many things you can do, you're more committed to the one or two things you *can* do. Today, those girls would have to weigh their ukulele-playing against Little League, gymnastics, computer camp, aerobics, shopping, and playing video games at the mall.

If you've ever had to find workers for church programs, you know that the church has to compete with the smorgasbord of activities people feel they must pursue. "I'd like to, but I'm already so busy" is a standard response to a request to work in the church. We've said it ourselves.

Sometimes the response is a cop-out and an excuse. Other times it's legitimate. All of us can't participate in all church programs, and we're not called or equipped to. We may have a ministry outside the programs of the church. Spending time with our family and carrying out a Christian witness at work will keep us occupied a good many hours. But if we never have time to minister in any way, we should ask ourselves if we're shutting the Lord out of our schedules. We can get too busy with things that won't last.

Older church members ask why we no longer have a huge youth group on Wednesday nights. They remember when the young people took the Sunday night service once a month, when the church was as full Sunday nights as it was Sunday mornings. Last Sunday the leader of the kids' club had to get up in church and nearly plead for workers. We're trying to schedule a home Bible study, but we are having a hard time finding a night when all the interested people are free.

Are the people in our church uncommitted to the Lord, indifferent about the Bible, uncaring about kids? No—but they are *busy*. They have to say no to church because they have already said yes to so many other things. Or they try to take on the church activities but find they're doing a halfhearted, last-minute job because they were tied up all week with miscellaneous other activities.

Trying to Do It All

We stated that today we have endless choices of what we will do with our lives. Perhaps it's more accurate to say we are expected not to choose between any of them but to do them all! Choosing means saying no to many things while we say yes to one thing; instead, we refuse to choose but try to do everything. God blesses choice-making; He gives us free will, which means He gives us the ability to choose. But He does not give us the ability (or the time or the money or the talent) to do everything.

No one likes to have to choose between two good things. We want them both. Having one means not having the other. Some of us need to learn the obvious lesson that we can't be two places at the same time, either physically or mentally. If the choir and the youth group meet at the same time, we'll have to choose between singing in the choir or helping with the youth group. If we try to do both (for example, leaving youth group early and getting to choir practice late), we'll find ourselves doing both halfway and neither one well.

Making a Choice

Once we get it through our heads that we have to choose among many good activities, how do we make that choice? We can look at our gifts and our energy level and notice if others are already doing the job better than we could. But there's another, deeper choice to make. It's a choice all of us are constantly making whether we realize it or not. It's the choice between Christ's kingdom and the world's kingdom.

"No one can serve two masters," Jesus said. "Either he will hate the one and love the other, or he will be devoted to the one and despise the other. You cannot serve both God and Money" (Matt. 6:24). It's impossible to simultaneously serve both the Lord and everything else in life that clamors for our attention, time, and energy. We cannot serve both God and work, or both God and leisure, or both God and social status or physical health or success. Above all, we cannot serve both God and our own desires in any form, even when they're expressed through our service to the church.

When the panorama of possible activities is spread in front of us, we must stop and ask what the Lord's will is in all of it. Some activities involve sin and can be discarded right away. Then the harder work comes: sorting out the best among all the good possibilities. Many things are wholesome but will take up time and energy we should spend on something better. In the smorgasbord of expectations (our own and other people's) we have to ask, "Which of these things does Christ want of me right now?"

We find it helpful to remember that as we think and dream of ministries we'd like to do, we sometimes see the present and the future at once and get them confused. Some of the good things which appeal to us may be meant for later on. Others may be for someone else to do while we pray or give our money or otherwise encourage them. We don't have to do everything; some of us even try to outdo God by expecting ourselves to do more than He wants or expects of us.

No matter how good an activity looks, we must consult the Lord through prayer and His Word before we commit ourselves to it. If we wind up doing it halfheartedly or sloppily, we aren't serving in His way no matter how good the plan looked at first. When we jump into an activity that isn't His will for us, we burn out from our own self-effort or quit before the job is accomplished or succeed but do it all for our own credit.

The search for credit for ourselves leads to a lot of empty activity. Sometimes it builds great buildings and makes money, but it is chaff in the Lord's eyes.

By the time we had been married three years, we had lived on the West Coast, the East Coast, and several countries in Europe, and we had been involved in a variety of ministries. A woman whose life had also been busy and varied said to Sandy, "Be careful you don't become a list of all the things you've done." It was good advice because it's tempting to tally up our accomplishments and say, "This equals me. Because I have done this, this, and this, I must be a valuable person."

God's Grace above Our Expectations

Romans 8 is a favorite chapter for those of us who get particularly frustrated with our personal inability to live up to what we think we should do or be. It's a chapter which brings us back to the sufficiency of the Holy Spirit in us. It's also a chapter which reminds us that Christ has already done everything necessary to bring us to God. The life which we continually try to live in our own power, He has already lived—and is still living—by His Spirit in us. He has done what our best efforts could never do: He has reconciled us to God and has fulfilled God's Law.

Our own failures point a finger at us and tell us we aren't good enough for God. And it's true; we aren't good enough. We're in willing rebellion against Him. Sometimes our rebellion takes the form of good works performed to get glory for ourselves when God has said, "I will not give my glory to another" (Isa. 42:8).

In Romans 7 we look in on Paul himself, the great apostle, facing up to his own sinful nature which sabotaged all his efforts at keeping the Commandments. He wrote, "I know that nothing good lives in me, that is, in my sinful nature. For I have the desire to do what is good, but I cannot carry it out" (Rom. 7:18).

Paul was in a great position to be idolized by other Christians in his own time and now. He could have glossed over his own sinful nature. But Paul didn't deny his sin and failure before God. Neither should we. The solution he found was to accept the merciful deliverance of Christ: "Therefore, there is now no condemnation for those who are in Christ Jesus, because through Christ Jesus the law of the Spirit of life set me free from the law of sin and death. For what the law was powerless to do in that it was weakened by the sinful nature, God did by sending His own Son in the likeness of sinful man to be a sin offering" (Rom. 8:1-3). By His death on the cross for us, Jesus has made up for our sins. The bad news is that nothing we do can ever make up for our sins; the good news is that it doesn't have to!

Still, self-effort and self-righteousness tempt us, even among those of us who say we are living in His grace. How often do we brag about our weaknesses? We usually conceal, deny, defend, or apologize for them. Paul's intention was to "boast all the more gladly about my weaknesses, so that Christ's power may rest on me" (2 Cor. 12:9).

The point is not that we are proud of our sins. The point is that our weaknesses and failings give God the opportunity to work in us and give us the opportunity to trust God. When we're weak, we know for sure that the Spirit carries us. "The Spirit helps us in our weakness. We do not know what we ought to pray, but the Spirit himself intercedes for us with groans that words cannot express. And he who searches our hearts knows the mind of the Spirit, because the Spirit intercedes for the saints in accordance with God's will" (Rom. 8:26-27).

God's grace is no excuse for halfhearted living or shoddy morals. But it does provide a place to stand when the ground of our own efforts has washed out from under us—as it will, eventually, sometime and somehow, no matter how talented or gifted we are.

We should prayerfully consider and evaluate the expectations others put on us, and we should do the same for the expectations we place on ourselves; but in the end, following Christ in our individual lives is the only way to discover who we're really supposed to be.

MESSAGE TWO:

Everything You Need Is Within You.

If you were asked to join an occult group you knew practiced witchcraft, you would run in the opposite direction. Unfortunately the practices and beliefs of the New Age Movement do not usually make themselves so obvious. Discerning the subtle influence of the New Age takes more than listening for a few buzzwords such as *global*, *networking*, and *wholistic*. As Christians, we must learn how to discern, analyze, and answer this newly prevalent philosophy in the light of Scripture.

Suppose you go to a self-help seminar and hear that you are in total control of your own life and can achieve anything if you believe it. Do you give it a try? Laugh? Feel like a flop if you can't do it? How do you sort out which parts of the seminar contain truth and helpful advice and which are lies?

Like New Agers, we like to think of ourselves as in control and as people without flaws. We are also tempted to make God in our own image and start acting like little gods.

Once we confess that we and New Agers share the same common human temptations, we can understand them and compassionately confront them with a positive Christian witness.

CHAPTER FOUR

You Can Control Your Own Life

Madeline was caught up in many quarrels: with the rules at her condominium, with her ex-husband who wouldn't pay child support, with her lawyer who wasn't on the ball. She was looking for a second lawyer to sue her first lawyer. She always turned down our invitations to church or Bible study. We noticed, however, that she became very interested when someone else began talking to her about out-of-body experiences, astral travel, and communicating with spirits.

When Madeline enthusiastically told us about a spiritist meeting she had recently attended, it seemed logical to ask her a question: "Since you're interested in all kinds of spiritual things, why won't you explore Christian beliefs as well? After all, Christianity has to do with the supernatural."

Madeline's answer was as blunt as it was profound. "Christianity teaches you to be a good person," she said. "But I'm already a good person. I want to know how to control my environment. These things I'm studying show me how I can be in control of my life."

Though she had a poor understanding of Christianity, which teaches us how to be saved from our sins and follow Christ rather than how to "be a good person," Madeline did have a handle on human nature's fundamental power drive. Most of us wouldn't dare put it as bluntly as she did, but wouldn't we like to be in control of the world? Maybe not the *entire* world but at least certain aspects of *our* world? Life would be less stressful, we could relax, we'd be a lot happier, if only we could make certain key parts of our lives behave themselves.

Fretting over the "If Onlys"

The unmanageability of life hits us on various planes. There are the great cosmic issues of war, poverty, and injustice, which we'd like to put an end to if we could. Then closer to home there are the mundane unmanageables, which actually occupy most of our fretting time.

"Less stress!" said a pharmacist we know, in a tone just short of a battle cry. "If I could just make life have less stress!" We can all sympathize. If only the car would quit dying at every red light, if only the kids would dress decently and start cleaning their rooms, if only the people who run the programs at church would do things the way we used to do them, if only my supervisor would finally notice how hard I work, and if only the neighbor across the street would keep his dog tied up—if these and a constellation of other events would only happen, then life would finally be manageable.

The Power We Crave

It ought to be obvious: *We are not in control of everything that happens to us.* Life itself should teach us that well. We do not have power over circumstances or other people. But *we want it*—and that seductive promise of power and control is exactly what made spiritualism so attractive to Madeline.

We Americans are eternal optimists. We are also insatiable consumers. When we have a lack in some area, we're confident that sooner or later somebody will find a solution and sell it to us at a price we can afford. Sure enough, now that we think we can and should have power over our lives, people are offering it to us. The drive for power has millions of ready customers.

Through work with DNA, scientists are more and more able to control the human organism. A generation or two ago, the view of a genetically engineered future controlled by white-coated scientists was chilling. But now genetic engineering is something *we* can do for ourselves, and that seems to make it OK. It is marketed as a useful service available to anyone who can pay for it. If Hitler were to do this to me, it would be terrible; if I can do this for myself or my children, it's wonderful. Superhuman control is fine as long as I'm the one in control. But the prospects are still chilling.

Alan Verhey writes of the dangers of genetic engineering:

Some people think of technology, including genetic technology, as society's toolbox. A new technology is just a new tool, an option for society to use or not as it sees fit. We will make what we want with it. Indeed, if we master enough tools, we may yet construct utopia. When technology fails, we will search for yet another tool to fix it. That view of technology is naive and, when applied to genetic engineering, dangerous. . . . Although technologies are introduced to make things we want, they seldom satisfy our wants. . . . If we can have a child when we could not have one before, we now want a particular kind of child, say a bright, blond boy. Technology is self-stimulating.... Although technology has brought real benefits, the confidence that it will always bring well-being (or that, if it doesn't, some new technology can correct the harm) is folly ("Society's Toolbox," *Christianity Today*, February 7, 1986, p. 27).

The right to abort a fetus would appear to put great personal power in the hands of women. Many stand up for "a woman's right to control her own body." A writer living in modern India warns:

Beware what you set your heart upon, for surely it shall be yours.... I say this as an American resident of India where an updated version of female infanticide is being practiced. Amniocentesis, a medical procedure used to detect certain fetal abnormalities, almost always reveals the sex of the unborn child—a side benefit doctors in India now put to use in a culture that prizes sons.... The basic principle of the abortion-on-demand movement is that the decision to abort should rest entirely with the woman.... Yet some mothers, indeed many mothers in India and other countries and cultures where males are highly prized, have very legitimate reasons in believing that giving birth to a girl is unacceptable. What gives anyone the right to tell them they are wrong? (Jo McGowan, "In India, They Abort Females," *Newsweek*, January 30, 1989, p. 12)

Flip through the ads in a news magazine this week. Take them all in at one shot. They look like something from an egomaniac's fantasies. They're selling technology, but their tone is ethereal, almost spiritual. They promise you—you personally, you ordinary, mortal human—everything but the ability to change the course of mighty rivers and leap tall buildings in a single bound. Look closer and they probably promise that too.

Here's a futuristic sunrise bursting with unspeakable energy, beckoning you to put yourself on the threshold of omnipotence—if you link up with a certain telephone system.

Here's the hand of God (oops, no, it's a computer salesman) offering you contact and influence in every corner of the known universe—if you buy into this computer system.

Here's a couple who has everything (project you and your mate into this picture) and are about to get even more—if they bank at the right bank, the one which gives them unlimited financial strength.

What sells things these days? The ads are transparent: it's the promise of power. They're not simply selling an efficient technology. They're saying: Do this, buy this, and you shall control things and get what you desire.

Do we naturally think we're supposed to control things and therefore we're drawn to these ads? Or do the messages tell us we're supposed to control things, and we choose to believe them? It's hard to say which is the cause and which is the effect. Certainly, human nature's basic power drive has been in us since we first fell into sin. What's different now is that the lust for power has a whole new image. It isn't a sin or a character fault. It's our right—no, our duty—to have power over our personal world.

The messages around us tell us we should have personal power over our circumstances, over other people, and over our own lives. If we do not have this power, we have no one to blame but ourselves. If we feel weak and powerless, that's the result of wrong thought patterns. We need to wake up to the power within us, take responsibility for our lives, take over, and put our personal power into action.

How appealing this sounds! It's even more appealing because it's somewhat based on fact. We *should* be responsible people. If we do something wrong, we should admit it. We should not blame others for the problems we cause ourselves. And we could all do more than we do. Few of us live up to our God-given potential. The Bible tells us that God "is able to do immeasurably more than all we ask or imagine, according to his power that is at work within us" (Eph. 3:20). If we trust Him and rely on His power, surely we will accomplish much good.

But what's being offered us by the world is very different from reliance on the power of God "who works in you to will and to act according to his good purpose" (Phil. 2:13). It's the urge to use the power of self instead—the same power that drove the first humans into the first sin in Genesis 3. The tempter said, "God knows that when you eat of it your eyes will be opened, and you will be like God, knowing good and evil" (Gen. 3:5).

Unbounded power—it's offered to us through a curious mix of technology and spiritism. Technology will put the world at our fingertips; benevolent spirit guides and the "perfect self" within us will show us the way to achieve all we perceive.

Promises of New Age Thinking

New Age thinking, which is rapidly flowing into the mainstream of American thought, preaches the inevitable upward progress of mankind. As we grow into harmony with the "God" in us and in the earth, we will create a humanitarian world of peace and freedom. But to accomplish this, we must all take control of our lives and act with the authority of the "God" within us. The New Age movement is a spiritualism which promises material gain and that elusive control over our world which Madeline longed for.

Christians do not need to fear New Age thinking, but we do need to have a good understanding of it in order to share the contrasting truths of the Scripture with the increasing number of people we'll meet who have bought into the New Age. There are many excellent books on New Age thinking: *Unmasking the New Age* and *Confronting the New Age* by Douglas R. Groothuis (InterVarsity) and *The New Age Rage* by Karen Hoyt (Fleming H. Revell); *The Universe Next Door* by James W. Sire (InterVarsity) is also helpful.

In addition to being knowledgeable about the New Age, we must also be aware of the danger of New Age thinking infiltrating our own view of the world. We don't need to go hunting for it; we hear it everywhere. It's preached by stars who urge ordinary people to share their "enlightenment," by management-seminar leaders who promise increased efficiency and productivity, by certain educators from pre-school through graduate school, and by some counselors.

The New Age is sorcery dressed up as science—spiritual manipulation of the world disguised in the respectable garments of good business, good counseling, and good education. Without witch-hunting, we must be on our guard to keep New Age thinking from entering our thinking as Christians.

New Age thinking is a Westernized, materialistic remake of ancient Eastern religions, which identify the human self as a part of God and God as the sum total of all that is. A series of well-known books and movies dramatizes the New Age's most famous practitioner as a saint on a pilgrimage to the truth that she is God and so is everybody else, a truth revealed to her through spirit guides and extraterrestrial beings.

Since we are God, this story line goes, we have no limitations. If we feel unconnected with God and if we fail at what we try to do, our problem is not sin or even weakness; it is lack of knowledge. If we will only realize and take action on the fact that we are part of God, we can literally do anything.

Such blatant egocentrism and disregard for God has had to dress itself up in benevolent neutrality in order to be respectable, but respectable it has become.

New Age Thinking: Solipsism's Cousin
New Age thinking is a second cousin to solipsism, the philosophy that I am the only thing which exists, and all the reality which appears to be "out there" is actually my own creation.

Solipsism seems to be a particular hazard of the junior high years. Since we work with young teens and write for them, the conversation in our home often turns to what it was like to be in junior high. Recently, several of our friends remembered some of their odd, teenaged perceptions about the nature of reality and the self.

"When I was in junior high I thought the outside world wasn't really there," Duane recalled. "I thought I was some kind of experiment. If my mother said it was time to get up and go to school, she wasn't really there, it was just a test to see what I'd do."

Marilyn agreed. "That's a lot like what I thought. I thought everything that seemed to be happening wasn't really happening—I was just making it all up inside my head. I was the only thing that was real."

The absolute self-centeredness in these statements is obvious. If I'm the only thing that exists, it doesn't matter what I do. There's nobody out there to tell me what to do or to see me do it.

We should be aware that the thinking of the New Age is sort of solipsism's cousin. New Age followers believe: *I create everything that happens to me. Reality is only what I perceive it to be. I make my own reality.* This kind of thinking leads to the conclusion that if I am wholly in control of my life, I have no one to blame but myself if something awful happens to me.

Now like all believeable lies, this one contains just enough truth to make it sound valid. We *are* to blame for *some* things that happen to us. For example, a friend of ours was depressed over a broken relationship. He went bar-hopping, got drunk, and tried to drive home. The next thing he knew, the police were pulling him out of a ditch and informing him he had been involved in a hit-and-run collision several miles back. He could have blamed the police, the other driver, the bartender, or that person who had walked out of his life. Instead, he said, "I did this to myself, and I'll take the consequences."

Fair enough. But what about the other driver who was innocently and legally pulling out onto the road? Was it her fault a drunk driver came along right then? The New Age says yes, she was absolutely responsible for what happened to her. She must have wanted it to happen because she is in control of her life, and everything that happens to her is what she wills to happen.

Imagine the guilt such thinking brings for those of us who find that, believe as we might, there are some things we cannot do. To a person with cancer, the New Age says, "Your cancer is a result of wrong thinking. You're doing this to yourself. Take control of your life." To a person in poverty the New Age says, "If you're poor, it's your own fault. If you only believe, you can lift yourself out of this condition and achieve anything you want to achieve."

Most of us could probably achieve more than we do. But

believe as we might, there will be things we cannot achieve. That isn't negativity or lack of faith. That is realism.

If you're a forty-year-old woman, you will never, never become an Olympic gymnast. Sorry. It's impossible, no matter how much you believe in yourself. If you take classes and work very hard, you may increase your strength and flexibility far beyond your expectations; you may even work up a fairly decent routine on the balance beam. But if you want to become an Olympic gymnast, you are about thirty-six years too late. Even if you once had the natural ability, you are now inescapably beyond hope of competing with fourteen-year-olds.

Letting God Run Our Lives

It's a theological issue. Who's writing the script for our lives? Are we the originators, authors, producers? Is it all up to us to decide what we're going to be and do it for ourselves?

Or is God the one who should order our lives? Is He the one we should go to and trust for guidance about what to do and be? Of course He is.

The Lord has not changed since He spoke through Isaiah: "I am the Lord, and there is no other. I have not spoken in secret, from somewhere in a land of darkness; I have not said to Jacob's descendants, 'Seek me in vain.' I, the Lord, speak the truth; I declare what is right. . . . Turn to me and be saved, all you ends of the earth; for I am God, and there is no other" (Isa. 45:18b-19, 22).

From Scripture we learn that God alone knows the truth, that God communicates His truth to us, and that only in Him will we find the power to live as we should. We can securely trust ourselves to a God who knows everything and can do everything. All other gods, especially the god of self, will fail us and ultimately destroy us.

Some people balk at the idea of letting God control their life. "What am I supposed to do when I wake up in the morning?" they ask. "Wait until God dumps me out of bed? Do I not make a move all day unless He pushes me? Do I go around listening for Him to tell me what to say? Don't I still have to go out and make a living, take care of my responsibilities? God's not going to do everything for me!"

Yes, there's some accuracy in those complaints. We don't physically feel God's hand getting us out of bed in the morning. We do have to start our cars and drive to work or the shopping mall. Money does not miraculously appear in our wallets. When we're faced with a difficult decision, we pray and read the Word and ask wise Christians, but we still have to make up our own minds.

Certainly God is not the Great Puppeteer who pulls our strings while we are passive. He does not want us to be lazy. "The sluggard buries his hand in the dish; he is too lazy to bring it back to his mouth" (Prov. 26:15). Obviously, God is not going to prop up the sluggard's hand and feed him; He wants this lazy person to take the initiative to feed himself. "A little sleep, a little slumber, a little folding of the hands to rest—and poverty will come on you like a bandit and scarcity like an armed man" (Prov. 24:33-34).

Then what does it mean to let God control our lives? It does not mean we become robots. It means we are open to following the leading and guidance of God. When we do what we do simply because He has told us to do it, then we are letting Him control us.

That requires surrendering our wills to Him. We must admit two very basic things: that the Lord is wiser than we are, and that we have a selfish drive to usurp His authority. When we consciously and daily yield our lives to Him, we open the door to letting Him control us.

Once we're in the pattern of surrendering our will, then we need to take the time to ask Him for guidance: "If any of you lacks wisdom, he should ask God, who gives generously to all without finding fault, and it will be given to him" (James 1:5). When we follow what He tells us to do, we're allowing Him to control us even though we must still put feet to our prayers and put into action what He has told us.

Obviously, once God has told us what to do, we need to do it. When we refuse to obey, then it's plain we're no longer letting Him control our lives. Obedience requires discipline: We do not naturally want to obey God. The book of Hebrews tells us the remarkable fact that even Jesus Christ in His earthly life had to learn obedience through discipline: "During the days of Jesus' life on earth, he offered up prayers and petitions with loud cries and tears to the one who could save him from death, and he was heard because of his reverent submission. Although he was a son, he learned obedience from what he suffered" (Heb. 5:7-8).

Learning to let God take control may be a difficult process, but God makes it worth it: "No discipline seems pleasant at the time, but painful. Later on, however, it produces a harvest of righteousness and peace for those who have been trained by it" (Heb. 12:11).

Yes, we still have to get up and go through our days under our own power. But when our natural strength is infused with God's power, in submission to God's power, the days are filled with joy, which the destructive control of Self can never offer.

CHAPTER FIVE

God Is Whatever You Think He Is

"Say, you people know a lot about the Bible! What do you think of this?"

It was one of those nights at Hardees. Sometimes we drop in for a late-night Big Cookie and coffee and don't see one person we know. Tonight, we were seeing all the people who feel compelled to tell us, immediately and intensely, why they don't believe like we do. In the guise of questions, of course.

"What do you think of this?" Gloria went on, leaning at us through the plastic plants. "Since God is the energy force in us, in every cell of our bodies, and we're one with God, then when you sin, you're actually sinning against yourself. What do you think of that?"

We had to admire Gloria's neat switch from "us" to "you" when the word *sin* came up. Gloria visits psychics for guidance, and her question was a heavy one to ask—or try to answer—late at night through a wall of plastic ivy. Especially when we'd just finished a half-flippant, half-serious conversation with Jack, who grew up in church but now venerates various "spirits in the earth" and says he prays to a god named Coyote. Jack had dived at us from an adjacent booth with the words, "Say, you people know a lot about the Bible! What do you think of all these TV-preacher scandals?"

Of course the Bible is not what Jack and Gloria really want to talk about—at least not yet. What they do want to talk about, long and intensely, are their own ideas about God. Though they're far from being Christians, they have their own definite ideas about who and what God is, and they're eager to talk about Him—or It.

Everyone wants to talk about God. Mention church and many people are bored; mention religion and they're cynical; even mention the Bible and they shy away. But mention God, and almost everyone is ready to talk. People answer the question "Who is God?" in all kinds of ways, but few people think it's a question not worth answering.

Stay at our local Hardees till after the bars close, and you'll hear even wilder ideas of who God is. "Tree-huggers" (an affectionate term for die-hard, back-to-nature buffs) talk about their experiences of "oneness with God" as they realize they are one with the lakes, stars, and loons, which are all "part of God." A woman into psychic healing talks about how God is the shifting energy force flowing through all of us and how our bodies heal themselves by moving this energy around. A former drinker tells us "the man up there" helped him quit drinking. Still others toss around God's name as a handy, all-purpose expression of anger, frustration, amazement, and all other convenient emotions.

We can't get away from God. He even bothers the people who don't think He exists.

Our friend Les, also a writer, invariably greets us with "Well, here come Dale and Sandy. We're on opposite sides, but they're OK." When Dale has called to invite Les to a

Bible study at our home, Les talks for twenty minutes about why he's a "nontheist" who has no interest in discussing the Bible. If he isn't interested in discussing it, why is he talking about it so much? Because he can't get away from God. None of us can. Even if we don't believe in Him, we feel compelled to talk about what we think of Him.

Warped Views of God

Is God one and the same with the atoms in our bodies or the spirits in the earth? Is He a nice guy? A judge? Is He benevolent or bestial or benign? Is He, as the Bible says He is, truly and fully revealed in Jesus Christ? The way we talk about Him reveals who and what we think He is—or what we'd like Him to be.

Strange views of God are everywhere. Consider these mesmerizing words quoted in *Family Circle* magazine:

Across the stream stands a tree, which attracts you because something there wants to talk to you. . . . You move closer toward a brilliant white light under the tree and you allow your higher self to emerge from it—meet it. . . . It is you. It has always been you, not only in this life but for as long as you lived. This is your real self. This is the personal God you have always wanted to meet (Laurie Nadel, "Shirley MacLaine: A Peek Inside Her Psychic Seminars," *Family Cirle*, October 1, 1987, p. 50).

This was spoken in the grand ballroom of a Boston hotel to an audience of 1,000 people.

"I've got to start going to church," our neighbor keeps saying, simultaneously turning down our invitations to come with us. "When I was a kid, my dad was out of work, and he went to church one Sunday and somebody offered him a job. So I know it works." Who is her God? He's a helpful fellow who rescues us when we're in extremities but who makes no demands. Right now she isn't quite at the extremity where she needs Him enough to seek Him out. She adds, "I'd like my kids to go to church." Apparently God is OK for the older and younger generations, but not for her. Not right now.

"God and I have an agreement," said an acquaintance of Sandy's. "He stays up there and I stay down here. I don't bother Him and He doesn't bother me." Perhaps that was a one-sided agreement. At any rate, these comments represent yet another view of God: He exists, but He'd better not impose His rules on my life.

We ask another acquaintance what he thinks of Jesus Christ. He answers, "I believe in Him. He's the Saviour. He's my ticket to heaven." This guy is living with his girlfriend, though she sometimes kicks him out when his drinking makes him violent. They just had a baby but have no plans to be married. He does not appear to be making any efforts to change his way of living. Yet he's counting on Jesus to be his ticket to heaven. His Jesus is merciful and asks no change of lifestyle.

In Sandy's college days she overheard one student telling another how he avoided the required chapel attendance: "I just told the dean, 'I know I've missed chapel a lot. But God understands.'" And both students burst out laughing. Their God was a joke, an excuse to manipulate their way around school rules.

All the concepts of "God" that our inventive friends manufactured contain a little bit of truth. God *is* our helper, and no doubt in His kindness He did give our neighbor's father that job and enable our alcoholic friend to quit drinking. God does understand our weaknesses and failings that might keep us from chapel or a thousand other responsibilities. It is true that Jesus died for those whose sins involve sex or alcohol—or any other sin. And He is present everywhere. He does welcome our prayers no matter how stumbling, and He does give us the free will even to tell Him to stay away. He even allows us to claim He doesn't exist.

The seed of accuracy in all these warped views of deity serves to show how the truth of God universally invades our human consciousness. In some form or other, we can't get away from Him. Nearly all of us, all over the world, all through history, have believed that there is some kind of God. And we apprehend much about Him simply from living in this world He has made, as Paul wrote in Romans: "What may be known about God is plain to them, because God has made it plain to them. For since the creation of the world God's invisible qualities—His eternal power and divine nature—have been clearly seen, being understood from what has been made, so that men are without excuse" (Rom. 1:19-20).

The New Age View of God
These days people are finding uniquely self-serving ways to answer that ever present question: Who is God? Rapidly entering the mainstream of our culture is a view of God so radically different from historical Christianity—and so stunningly seductive—that all Christians should be aware of it and prepared to deal with it.

In the previous chapter we talked some about the New Age movement's view of God. New Agers use the word *God* in an unbiblical way but also in a very attractive way. God is not denied or downgraded in the New Age. "God" is presented as something good, powerful, and desirable. However, this is no picture of the biblical God. Since it's increasingly necessary for us to have an active dialogue and witness to New Agers, we must understand what they mean when they refer to "God." Otherwise we'll assume they mean what Christians mean simply because we both use the same word.

The New Age says that "God" is ultimate reality, and ultimate reality is "God." "God" is everything there is. "God" is All.

On the surface that sounds fine. Don't we even sing songs that say "He's everything to me" and "Jesus is all the world to me"? Scripture says that "in Him all things hold together" (Col. 1:17) and praises "one God and Father of all, who is over all and through all and in all" (Eph. 4:6). But the simple words *one* and *all* take on very different meanings in Christianity and in the New Age.

Christianity begins with the biblical premise that God is the basis of all reality; it assumes a personal God who has created all else and who would exist even if He never created anything. New Age thinkers begin with a concept of all reality and then call it "God."

New Age Reality

Just as our Christian view of God as a loving and righteous Father determines how we live and relate to Him, the New Age view of reality determines everything else in the movement's doctrine and agenda.

What's "real" to the New Age? First of all there is the basic conviction that *everything is one*. Sounds innocuous at first, doesn't it? Of course everything is one—there is only one everything; there aren't two everythings. But there's more to "all is one" than the external language lets on at first.

What is this "all" the New Age reveres? It is not, as Christians use it, a metaphor for "my entire meaning of life" or "my ultimate source of strength." "All" means literally everything. Everything: earth, heaven, plants, animals, rocks, stars, you, me. "God" is the impersonal unity of all that is.

"All is one" means that all apparent distinctions between anything and anything else are illusory. There is no distinction between good and bad, between life and death, between earth and heaven, between you and me, between "God" and creation. There is even no distinction between "God" and you. You are part of "God." You are literally "God," with no barriers or limitations to your potential. In other words, you can do anything. You are limited only by ignorance and incorrect thinking. Straighten out your thinking by New Age enlightenment, and your life will know no boundaries. Sickness, mortality, moral law, values, or even death will have no claim on you.

Our Shifting Cultural Reality

How our culture's assumed basis of reality was reversed in only a couple of decades ought to go down in history. A concept of God and reality which would have been ridiculed in the U.S. in 1790, 1890, and even 1970 is becoming gospel in 1990. How did it happen? There are many reasons. Many people who embraced an anti-materialist occultism in the 1960s have become the teachers, counselors, managers, and media experts who now exercise tremendous influence on how our society thinks. And they haven't altered their philosophy simply because they have aged and cut their hair. Then there's the natural pendulum swing away from the possessive "me first" seventies and eighties to a new interest in spirituality and a hunger for spiritual guidance.

Most of all, this new, cultural reality denies the existence of the real God revealed in the Bible and emphasizes our insatiable desire to replace God with our own gods made in our own image. Our natural hostility toward God, which is the essence of sin, is what ultimately gives the New Age a foothold in our thinking.

There's nothing new about any of this. Rebellion against God is the problem we've had since the beginning when mankind first fell into sin, as recorded in Genesis 3. It will be with us until Christ returns. Christ offers forgiveness for sin, and the Holy Spirit offers to renew us from within and help us overcome sin, but we'll always need to be on our guard against the tendency to replace God with gods in our own image.

Adam and Eve had been taught by God firsthand what He wanted them to know about Himself and the consequences of choosing or not choosing Him. But there came a moment when the serpent's temptation was more attractive to Eve than all that God Himself had taught her. The serpent was telling her what she wanted to be true: she and Adam would be OK, even better, if they disobeyed God; God is an understanding fellow anyway whose warnings are not to be taken seriously, and it was up to her to get for herself what God would deny to her and Adam.

The God of the Bible

Our friend Jack's nature-spirit, Coyote, is handy for spiritual guidance and empowerment, but he makes no moral demands on Jack. Gloria's energy force is ever present but impersonal, leading to no convictions about right and wrong and therefore no change in living habits. In both cases, "God" leaves them free to do as they please—in a sense, to be "God" themselves. Madeline, whom we mentioned in the last chapter, wanted more than freedom for herself; she wanted total control over others. No wonder she rejected Christianity, which promised her no such control or freedom. Christ makes no apologies about asking us to yield control of ourselves to Him and give up our freedoms for the sake of others.

We've noticed that people like Jack and Gloria, who have deliberately rejected what the Bible says about God, also have a compulsion to let us know that their ideas don't agree with the Bible. The Bible troubles them. Much as they want to write it off, their church backgrounds taught them too much about its power. Its quiet, age-old authority haunts their consciences.

What does the Bible say about God?

First, the Bible assumes He exists as an all-powerful personal Being. It does not attempt to prove His existence, though along the way it invites us to look at the evidence. The first sentence of the Bible starts out, "In the beginning God . . ." (Gen. 1:1). There is not a trace of argument or apology or explanation for this truth; it simply is because He simply is.

The Bible continues, "In the beginning God created the heavens and the earth." The natural world had a beginning, and God was already there when it happened. He made it happen. He *existed* before He brought the natural universe into being. He *will exist* after "the heavens will disappear with a roar; the elements will be destroyed by fire, and the earth and everything in it will be laid bare" (2 Peter 3:10). Though we perceive "God's invisible qualities" in "what has been made" (Rom. 1:20), in no sense does the Bible equate God the Creator with His creation.

Besides being the Creator, God is holy. He is perfectly righteous and set apart from us. He told His people, "Be holy because I, the Lord your God, am holy" (Lev. 19:2). They were to demonstrate their holiness to the pagan nations around them by living according to God's standards for morality, cleanliness, and fair play. But they were fully able to rebel and be unholy.

We are still fully able to do that. Even as we deal with New Agers and others about what the Bible says about God, we find in ourselves the same rampant power struggle.

This week we're going to see Les. He wouldn't come to Bible study, but he wants to talk about the supposed contradictions in the Bible. He seems to have made a career out of finding them. What will our attitude be as we talk with him? Will we get mad if he doesn't listen? Will we be thinking so hard about how we can get him to agree with us that we shut out Les, the real person? What about the New Age dabblers we know who refuse to come to Bible study? Do we want them to come to Bible study so we can feel good about the ministry we're having or because we genuinely love them and want them to come into relationship with God through Jesus Christ? We must see them not as victims to conquer but as vulnerable human beings who need God.

Living in God's Power

Recently some Christian friends were discussing how powerless they feel in the face of spiritual opposition. They longed for more power in prayer, in witness, in the realm of spiritual authority over evil. We want to feel powerful and competent in the face of wrong. But even as we ask the Lord for more power, we must be on our guard against the temptation to use His power for personal gain. Often we are actually most powerful, in Christ's power, at the very moment we feel the weakest.

Paul asked the Lord for relief from an affliction which harassed him. No doubt he felt it limited his ministry and effectiveness for the Lord. Perhaps he told the Lord how much more fruitful he could be if only the affliction were removed. Paul later reported, "Three times I pleaded with the Lord to take it away from me. But he said to me, 'My grace is sufficient for you, for my power is made perfect in weakness.' Therefore I will boast all the more gladly about my weaknesses, so that Christ's power may rest on me" (2 Cor. 12:8-9).

We all need discernment from the Lord when we're dealing with our own selfish drive to run things. And we need each other to point out in love the mistakes we're blind to. There is a subtle difference between trusting God to control circumstances and using God to manipulate circumstances for our benefit. It may be a small difference in how we pray but a great difference in our intentions and the implications of our prayers.

In the end, recognizing our own natural drive to control things can make us compassionate toward New Agers and others who want to remake God in their own image. Christians, New Agers, nontheists, and all others who labor under the burden of humanness are struggling with answers to very personal questions: Who's going to run my life? Who tells me what to do? In whose hands is it safe to place my life? As Christians, we answer those questions with "Christ" and explain that He has shown Himself to be a good and faithful Lord.

Les the nontheist wouldn't come to our Bible study, but he was glad when we offered to come to his place and talk about the Bible. He says he wants to discuss the supposed contradictions in the dietary laws between Leviticus and Deuteronomy. Now that's obviously a smoke screen. Nobody wants to sit around talking about the contradictions in the dietary laws between Leviticus and Deuteronomy. Well, there may be some people who do, but Les probably isn't really one of them. Why does he want to grab at that? He hopes it's a handle on the axe by which he can chop down the Bible. He wants to find contradictions, any contradictions, by which he can prove the Bible has no claims on him.

And Les is a loner around town. He will appreciate the company, even from somebody who is "on opposite sides" from him. When we go see him later this week, it won't really be to talk about dietary laws. It will be to talk about him and why he is so set on not believing as well as what the Bible says which he finds so distasteful. With time and prayer, perhaps even Les will give up playing God and come into relationship with the real God, not made with human hands or minds but alive before the beginning.

CHAPTER SIX

You Are "God"

"Rebirth ... wholeness ... inner transformation ... unshakeable confidence ... the law of believing ... winning relationships ... unlimited benefits ... inner peace and harmony ... no worries, doubts, and fears."

The promises almost sound like they come from Scripture. Is this an advertisement for an evangelistic crusade? It is, in a way, but the "evangelist" is preaching a different "gospel" from the Good News of Christ. The slick flyer in our mailbox is an ad for a set of self-help tapes, a condensation of a $5,000 seminar which promises all the above benefits and more.

How are we supposed to come into all this effulgent good fortune? There's no claim that the tapes alone will do it. According to the advertisement, the source of all these promised good things is that untapped well of wisdom, that origin of all goodness, that spring of latent power—the Self.

The *Self?* Whose self? Surprisingly, it isn't even the self of the seminar leader, though he must be fulfilling his own glittering promises of success if he gets $5,000 per seminar participant. No, the Self he says he wants to put you in touch with, who will give you all you've ever wanted and more, is your *own* self.

Yes, believe it or not, you are the source of all the good things you want. You are the untapped well of wisdom, the origin of all goodness, the spring of latent power—if only you will recognize it, believe, and master the techniques to begin to act like who you really are.

The message is a boost to a bruised ego! Are you feeling inadequate? Fenced in? Tied down? Frustrated? You can turn on these tapes and discover that all your limitations are an illusion. Here's "positive self-image" carried to the maximum! Realize that your true Self can do absolutely anything and then start doing it.

What Is Self?

Self is powerful. No matter what we think of Self, we can't be neutral about it. Our dictionary includes a solid page of hyphenated words beginning with *self-*, and it's interesting how each word has instant emotional content. Some of the *self* words make us think Self is a positive entity—words such as *self-consistent* and *self-employed.* Other words, such as *self-condemnation* and *self-doubt,* bring up the image of unfortunate mistreatment of poor Self. *Self-abandonment* and *self-forgetful* are positive to our ears, though (is this self-contradictory?) they make Self sound like something best gotten rid of.

Another category of *self* words instantly irritates us: *self-pity, self-gratification, self-importance,* and *self-appointed.* In all those words Self stands up for itself, and we want to punch it in the nose for all its self-absorption.

Is the true Self perfect? Is it even good? Or is it something to be abased?

For all our desire to find ultimate meaning in ourselves and better ourselves, few of us want to be labeled self-centered or selfish.

Yet many of us could use a more positive view of who we are and what we can do. Self-condemnation and self-hatred are signs of emotional sickness, not health. So the message of the advertised tapes appeals to our natural desire to feel good about ourselves.

At the same time, our experience with ourselves tells us Self is an unlikely candidate for deification.

Self is famous for getting us into trouble by bringing us into conflict with other selves. Self prefers to listen to itself instead of to God. Self makes us self-defensive and self-indulgent, and Self naturally spurns self-control.

The seminar leaders exaplain: "That's your ignorant, *unenlightened* Self. Your higher Self, your true, perfect Self, has been stifled by wrong thinking and social conditioning. You have spent your life being shaped by rational Western culture to believe wrong beliefs. Your thinking is splintered because you believe in physical limitations, rationality, traditional right and wrong, and so forth. You must realize that you are a manifestation of the All in which there is no flaw or lack. When you unleash your limitless inner powers, you'll realize you are perfect just the way you are."

Self Is "God"
The advertised tapes are not some odd aberration out of the lunatic fringe. Their message is common today. It finds a willing audience because the message that Self is "God" is a message Self loves to hear.

If the popularity of New Age self-help seminars is any indication, our society thinks Self needs a lot of help. The religion of Self as "God" is widespread, holding out the lure of limitless personal power through the realization that we are one with God. We are urged to look within ourselves to get all we need and want. No other source of values or guidelines is valid for us except our own personal experience (and, of course, the authoritarian pronouncements of the teachers and writers).

Even in the Bible school class Sandy helped with this summer in our conservative traditional town, one kid showed up wearing a sweatshirt from Maharishi International University, the Iowa center of meditation-based capitalism. ("My parents went there," she explained.)

If all the advertised potential for wholeness, peace, and prosperity guaranteed in these seminars and books were actually unleashed, the world ought to be transformed into a place of harmony, health, and plenty. But this power is not intended for the good of the world. Forget using your newfound omnipotence to develop new ways to feed and clothe the hungry. The seminars are *personal* achievement seminars, not seminars to help the underprivileged, who apparently must wait till they can afford the seminars before they can advance.

As the promotion of self has become increasingly important and acceptable, people have looked less at changing the world around them and more to what they can get, do, and achieve.

Seize this power, the message goes, so you can make money and control others and live more comfortably than your wildest dreams. The means are spiritual but the goal is material: business success, better sales, higher employee productivity. The hook is the promise of attaining personal desires. You have no responsibility to care for suffering people because those who are poor must want to be poor, and those who are sick must want to be sick. That's the logical result of the deification of Self.

To a Christian, the use of power for Self seems to contradict the New Age promise of an ever-upward progress toward personal perfection. People who are getting more selfish are going down, not up!

New Age Thinking in the Mainstream

The message of Self as "God," which is a religious message, enters our mainstream institutions disguised as good education and good business. When its practitioners become teachers or counselors or managers, they do not give up their philosophy any more than any Christian who enters those fields gives up faith in Christ. Chances are increasing that you'll encounter New Age faith in the office or in the classroom.

According to author Douglas Groothius, "Marilyn Ferguson notes that of 'the Aquarian Conspirators' she surveyed in her book, *The Aquarian Conspiracy*, 'more were involved in education than in any other single category of work. They were teachers, administrators, policymakers, educational psychologists.' Many complained they could not fully apply their Aquarian agenda, but they have been making progress" (*Confronting the New Age*, InterVarsity Press 1988, p. 129).

Even as we point out possible places you'll encounter New Age ideas, let us caution against being an alarmist or a finger-pointer. We need not see red flags in every use of the words *networking* or *global* or *vision*. Wisdom will lead us to identify and witness to New Agers, never to dismiss and condemn them. The New Age is wrong not because it's the New Age, but because its assumptions about truth contradict God's revealed truth in Scripture. Christians should be examining and debating presuppositions, not attacking personalities.

New Age deification of Self has come into some schools through teachers who urge students (even very young children) to consult with their perfect inner selves for answers to problems. In values clarification classes, young people are told to choose their own values, which are inherently right for them. This logic is not something a parent or teacher can really live with. Take a thirteen-year-old boy who is immersed in heavy metal music, beginning to use drugs, and regularly skips school to hang out with older boys who steal cars for joyrides. He may accurately clarify his current values as "freedom from restraint," "enjoying things that make adults nervous," and "being accepted by older males." Is the most devoted disciple of New Age autonomy willing to let him go at that? Any responsible adult cries out to offer guidance to such a kid. Yet values clarification classes tell us we must keep our hands off. They promote inherent, unquestioned moral autonomy.

Discernment is needed here. We all want our Christian young people to come to their own mature conclusions about right and wrong rather than parroting what their churches or parents have told them. Faced with the temptation to have sex or steal or cheat in school, remembering that "My Sunday School teacher said not to" won't be enough for them. Sunday School teachers thoughtfully instruct young children about Jesus in the Bible, but their greatest joy is to see a child come to his or her own personal faith. Of course we want young people to know their own values and stand up for them. But the move to maturity of personal belief is very different from urging teens to invent their own values and call them good.

In addition to a New Age influence in education, counseling is another area where we are likely to encounter the New Age. If we go to anyone for counseling—for career, education, marriage, or personal problems—we may be persuasively told that we have to develop our own values without regard to any outside influence since we are accountable only to ourselves. Again, we must be discerning. We may need help and have a limited choice of counselors to go to. Trained Christian psychologists or marriage counselors are not available everywhere. We can learn from non-Christians who understand the workings of the mind and emotions, but we must weigh their advice against Scripture (just as we must weight any Christian counselor's advice against Scripture). Counseling, like education, can never be neutral or value free. People are not likely to become counselors unless they have an image of the goals and values toward which they want to steer others. We have the right and the responsibility to know what those goals are before we accept counsel.

Then there's the marketplace. New Age spirituality is lavish in its promise of material gain, and there is now a profusion of management consultants who offer to guide workers toward greater effectiveness and harmony. The author of a *Newsweek* article explains:

> Goodbye Dale Carnegie. Hello Werner Erhard. The New Age movement has gone corporate. Faced with increased competition and sluggish growth, American companies are hiring motivational gurus to change the way their employees think. Besides Pacific Bell, such corporate giants as Procter & Gamble, TRW, Ford Motor Co. and Polaroid have all signed on New Age consultants (Annetta Miller with Pamela Abramson "Corporate Mind Control," *Newsweek*, May 4, 1987, p. 38).

Businesspeople are not accustomed to evaluating management or sales practices philosophically. Making money is the bottom line, and what works best is what will be put into practice. If employees can be spurred to greater productivity with increased motivation and more job satisfac-

tion, let's do it. The means (meditation, "internal align-
ment," mysticism) go unquestioned. The aim of the training
is to organize employees' thinking around certain fundamental values so that their goals are shared. Workers who
object to the training on religious grounds may be out of
luck—and out of work. Even the management of stress in
the workplace may include spiritual meditation and con-
trolling inner energy fields—clearly religious teachings
dressed up as good business.

The Biblical View of Self

This materialistic mysticism actually appeals to something
in all of us. Unless we understand our sinful nature, we
won't understand why others are drawn into the New Age,
and we will think ourselves immune from its appeal.

Let's look closely at the Self. This Self which is sold as
all-knowing and all-powerful is also a pain. We are tired
after a single day of dealing with ourselves. If we're sensi-
tive to our true selves, we know how our true selves are
naturally set against God.

You drag your Self out of bed to report to work when
your Self wants to sleep in. You bite your tongue when
your Self wants to snap back at a family member. You take
time to express concern for a neighbor when your Self
would rather be watching a sitcom. Or maybe you give in
to Self and are late for work, nasty to the family, and
uncaring to the neighbor. Either way, doesn't your experience so far today already tell you that your Self often
wants to do what's sinful?

Self is self-centered. God calls us to be God-centered
instead. Self-deification, far from being our salvation, is the
essence of sin.

In Christ we have a right to feel good about who we are.
We're God's beloved creations. The Bible says God created

us in His own image, a distinction He gave none of the plants and animals (Gen. 1:26-27). He honors us by giving us His Spirit (Eph. 1:13; 1 Cor. 12:13). He shares Himself with us in the intimacy of prayer, inviting us to approach Him (Heb. 4:16). He paid us the ultimate compliment when He even "became flesh and lived for a while among us" (John 1:14), and Scripture is clear that He did this because He loved us too much to let us die spiritually (John 3:16). He desires us to be with Him forever (John 17:24). These Scriptures and many others give us a picture of the human race as infinitely valuable to God.

At the same time, Jesus, who knows us better than anybody, warned us against the seductiveness of our Selves. He even made surrendering the Self a prerequisite of following Him. "If anyone would come after me, he must deny himself and take up his cross and follow me" (Matt. 16:24; Mark 8:34). Luke 9:23 adds the word *daily* to the explanation of self-denial.

If the Self is the wellspring of all happiness and peace of mind, why does Jesus tell us to say no to it every day? And why does the Self continually get us into trouble?

To be told by a self-help seminar that "you are God" is no help to you at all. In fact, to be told you are God is to destroy you. To believe you are God is to destroy yourself.

The message implies that believing we are all part of God will unify us. The fruit of the message is the opposite. We wind up a bunch of miniature gods running around pursuing our own agendas without regard for anyone else. Imagine the chaos such a pursuit causes. Well, we don't have to imagine it; we can observe it in our own society. We are a splintered collection of little gods trying to exert our power over each other while chasing our own comforts. We're out of harmony with each other, ourselves, and the real God who made us.

Needed: A New Self

The New Age says we need a better understanding of the Self. The Bible says we need a "new self, which is being renewed in knowledge in the image of its Creator" (Col. 3:10).

The need for a new birth does not mean we should despise our old selves. The Bible never downgrades the worth of human beings. If Christ considers us worth dying for, we must be tremendously valuable to Him. His death proves that He loves us (1 John 4:9-10). As we contemplate ourselves, we can be sure that we are very important to God.

Yet His death proves something else in addition to His love for us: it proves the depth of our sin. Our rebellion against God is so great that the Son had to pay for it with His own perfect life. Our drive to glorify Self cost Jesus His life to reunite us with God. Our bent toward sin was complete. God even had to take the first step toward us. Mankind was not on the way back to God when Jesus came; God had to take the initiative to save us.

It's no surprise that we have invented millions of ways to try to deny sin. We all try to get out from under it because we are all guilty of it. "There is no difference, for all have sinned and fall short of the glory of God" (Rom. 3:22-23). Sin gets laughed at by anyone who prefers to believe we're each a law unto ourselves. Sin gets ridiculed as an out-of-date concept, a relic from a repressive time, a tool of religious manipulation. But sin is still the best explanation for why our Selves, made in the image of a holy and loving God, continually cause turmoil and conflict. We are deliberately contradicting the purposes of God for ourselves.

That's the human dilemma: we demand our own way instead of God's way; we demand our Selves to be God instead of Him. No amount of enlightenment and education can reverse the trend begun with original sin. The very first sin was a brazen attempt to supplant God, and the essence of sin hasn't changed.

Here is a problem no set of $5,000 tapes can solve, even at their bargain price of $29.95 with a thirty-day guarantee. Knowledge alone will not save, not even knowledge of the Self. In fact not even knowledge of God's Law will save. God gave His written Law to one group of people, the Jews, and to everyone else He gave "the requirements of the Law ... written on their hearts" (Rom. 2:15). But the purpose of His law is to show us how far we are from His perfection and how much we need His salvation. "Through the Law we become conscious of sin" (Rom. 3:20). "So the Law was put in charge to lead us to Christ that we might be justified by faith" (Gal. 3:24). Jesus clashed with many learned people who made a speciality of studying the Torah, God's Law. They knew everything there was to know about God, but they refused to recognize and submit to Him when He came to them in the flesh.

We need forgiveness and renewal, not enlightenment. And that is what God ultimately provided for mankind. Christ did on the cross what learning and enlightenment could never do. He did not deify the human Self; He made a way for us to crucify the Self.

Steeped in a culture of the wrong kind of self-love, it's difficult for us to see how radically different is His message from that of the world. Paul wrote, "I have been crucified with Christ and I no longer live, but Christ lives in me. The life I live in the body, I live by faith in the Son of God, who loved me and gave Himself for me" (Gal. 2:20). Hardly an elevation of an all-powerful Self. Because of his surrender to Christ, Paul could also truthfully write, "I can do everything through Him who gives me strength" (Phil. 4:13). The *Him* he meant was not Paul but Jesus.

All Have Sinned

The New Age claims sin is an illusion, and Scripture responds, "If we claim to be without sin, we deceive ourselves and the truth is not in us" (1 John 1:8). That's the bad news. Whenever we share the Good News with anyone, we have to include the bad news. The task takes boldness and tact because no one wants to hear bad news, especially about something so personal as his or her own Self. But there is also overwhelmingly Good News: "If we confess our sins, he is faithful and just and will forgive us our sins and purify us from all unrighteousness" (1 John 1:9).

Here is a call for compassion and tenderness toward anyone caught in the New Age trap. We are all, Christians and non-Christians, in the same boat. The boat is christened Sin. We have all deified Self. Perhaps we do it in subtle, socially acceptable ways. Perhaps we even do it through religious means at church. Self is everyone's problem. All of us who know the Lord also know the selfishness of our own hearts.

We have entered into Christ's forgiveness, and we must invite others to do the same. At the same time we must stay aware of the deception of self-will which may invade even our witnessing efforts and all other areas of our lives. Every day, as we take up the cross of self-denial and follow Christ, we can be grateful to God again for His undeserved mercy. And we can repeat after Paul the words of Romans 7:25: "Thanks be to God—through Jesus Christ our Lord!" while acknowledging, "So then, I myself in my mind am a slave to God's Law, but in the sinful nature a slave to the law of sin." Until Christ takes us to be with Him, either by death or by His return, the battle with Self will continually cast us back on His mercy.

MESSAGE THREE:

Life Should Be Comfortable.

Most of us would agree that life should be comfortable. The problem is that life is often uncomfortable for us and the people we love.

Can we find value in suffering pain, enduring unfairness, and coping with the frustration of just waiting? Is there a reason to stick with someone or something that is no longer fun simply because we promised and because we are still needed? The Bible clearly answers yes to these questions and assures us that God has not left us alone in our pain.

CHAPTER SEVEN

No One Should Have to Endure Pain

Seven-year-old Ryan was diagnosed with a terminal disease five years ago. Years of therapy have produced temporary remissions but no cure. For a long time Walt, Ryan's father, was angry—angry at life, angry at God, and angry at himself for not being able to handle it all. He could not understand how a good and just God could allow this to happen. His anger at life damaged his relationships with people as they shied away from him, and his anger at God made him fear he had lost his salvation.

Finally, after Ryan had yet another setback, Walt admitted his own helplessness and surrendered the entire situation to God. Though he didn't understand what was happening, Walt took refuge in the Lord. Whether he lived or died, Ryan belonged to the Lord, and his future either way was in God's care.

Walt was a transformed person. For the first time in years he had peace. It was a glow that lasted—for a while. A few weeks later, Ryan's parents took him to one more specialist. Like the other doctors, this specialist said they had reached the end of the road medically; there was no hope. But by this time Walt and his wife had come under the influence of friends who insisted that Jesus would heal Ryan if only the church body had enough faith. God had absolutely promised healing in His Word, they said.

Last Sunday Walt stood up in church (a church in which signs and wonders have never been given star billing) and told the people that Ryan's healing was now up to God—*and them*. The Holy Spirit wanted to heal Ryan, but He could do it only in response to the church's faith. In a voice intense with emotion, Walt said, "There's nothing more the doctors can do. This church body has got to pull together and pray in faith because my son's life depends on it."

From all the evidence, Walt is completely right that only God can make Ryan well. But there are all kinds of other questions involved here: Did God promise wellness? If so, how much faith does He require to do what He has promised? Who is required to have faith—the sick person? his family? the entire church? What is God's timetable for healing? When He doesn't heal, why doesn't He? Does it also take faith to trust Him even when there is no healing? And is it also an act of faith to accept death as an inescapable part of the sin-broken human condition?

Those are reasonable questions. But how do you talk about them rationally in the midst of a life-and-death situation, which for five years has worn away at the emotions of the parents and the church and the family and Ryan himself? Here, mixed up and overlapping, are all the raw irrational feelings of parenthood, loss, fear, the suffering of innocent children, faith, pain, illness, and the promises of God. And it's all being played out within earshot of the ticking clock of terminal disease.

God is trustworthy, and His promises in Scripture are true. We may have read them with cool detachment in

Bible studies, but in times of intense emotional distress and need, we grab for them. So our interpretations of His promises are chronically filtered through our own desperate desires, wants, feelings, and needs. And therein lies both the Christian's hope and a potential trap for disappointment.

Comparing notes after church, both of us reported a creepy, cold feeling brought on by Walt's announcement. This may be only the beginning of a church conflict over whether the Lord promises healing in all cases, and it isn't the first time we have seen it. Do we want Ryan to die? Of course not. Do we want him to be healed? Of course we do. Will we pray that God heals him, either through medicine or a miracle? Of course we will—and have been all along. But will we pray for Ryan's healing in absolute confidence that God has promised it, prepared to take on incalculable guilt if it doesn't happen? We can't. We have seen too many faithful Christians die unhealed (or rather, be healed by being promoted to heaven), and we see too many suffering saints in the Bible to believe that the Lord will remove pain simply because we pray for it.

But how will we ever explain that to Walt if he asks us to pray in absolute faith for Ryan's healing? We'll be accused of disbelieving God's promises. That's how sure he and his friends are that physical healing is something God has promised every believer.

Latching onto Promises

We all want promises to be true. We want the security of knowing that the good fortune someone holds out to us is really going to be ours.

We don't have to go to church to hear promises. We hear promises everywhere, holding out hope for both our secular and our spiritual life. We naturally latch onto them, especially when they tell us what we want to believe.

A recent issue of a magazine advertises "books that heal" and a book that is "guaranteed to improve your performance in *everything* you do." An ad for tapes promises, "Use your mind to do anything you choose." Sample tape titles promise to tell you "How to Attract Money," "How to Be Happy," and the secrets of "Attracting More Love." Another tape ad makes its promise more cautiously in the form of a question: "Is it now actually possible to release the genius within you?" The tape titles are not so cautious: "Unlimited Mental Abilities," "Financial Success & Prosperity," "Awaken the Winner Within." (*Psychology Today*, June 1988, pp. 1, 7; September 1988, pp. 29, 61.)

Well, who wouldn't want to believe such promises? When your arthritis flares up again and your children are rebelling and your business is failing and your good friends are getting divorced and your church is going through a split, who doesn't want to be able to say, "There's got to be a cure for all this!" If a solution is vowed to exist, who wouldn't want to go looking for it?

If all the promises we hear were true, we should be enjoying a pain-free world. The messages of problem-free living with which our culture surrounds us are so persuasive and so lavish in their guarantees of solutions that when our problems don't go away, we think it's our fault. We must be doing something wrong.

End headaches instantly with this pill. Smooth family tensions with this approach. Relax your body and mind with this technique. Get your life under control with this time management plan. Keep your spouse faithful with these rules for a successful marriage.

The promises work—sometimes. Just like life works comfortably for us—sometimes. We can thank God for life-saving medical developments and for wise counsel in areas such as marriage and work. But no medical miracle yet has made mankind immortal, and no counsel cures forever the day-to-day friction of living and working with other fallen human beings.

Human promises come true part of the time. God's promises always come true. Then how do we understand what God has actually promised? As we search the Scriptures desperately for reassurance that everything will be OK, how do we differentiate between what He means and what we are reading into His Word?

If we believe in an all-powerful God who loves us, we naturally want to believe that He has promised to fix everything bad that happens to us or (preferably) save us from suffering in the first place. He wants what's good for us, and if we believe, He will do what's good for us. And we naturally believe we can identify what's good—in other words, we know what He should do.

There is such a ruthless logic here that we are shocked when problems continue despite how faithfully we resort to the cures. A woman whose husband had been unfaithful began to rigorously apply the principles she learned at a Christian family-living seminar. "I thought if I did everything right, my husband would stay faithful to me," she said later. But in spite of all her rightness, he was still free to go wrong—which he did again.

Searching for the Solution
Our culture conditions us to be intolerant of pain, whether mental, physical, emotional, or spiritual. We are taught to be impatient with difficulty. We are not encouraged to look for any use or purpose in it but to rid ourselves of it as soon as possible.

When comfort is our highest value, anything that makes us uncomfortable should be done away with immediately.

Because it causes discomfort, there can be no good in it.

We speak of how people "get old and die." But statistics show that before 1900, most people in this country did not get old and die. They died young instead. Or they died in middle age. Statistically, it was unusual for people to get old at all. To expect to live into one's eighties and maintain health and vigor would be asking for a miracle. Now, because of stunning medical advances, even Christians consider good health and long life our guaranteed rights. If something threatens our rights, we are incensed. And we immediately launch a search for the solution which *has* to be out there.

For Christians, the solution is of course Jesus. But there is always the temptation to treat Jesus as Superman, a hero who rescues us from problems we can't solve and then flies off, leaving us dazzled but morally unchanged. Jesus sees the value of our struggles and in many cases leaves us in them, sustained by His grace, to learn how to respond as He would respond.

We have plenty of scriptural examples of people the Lord rescued from trouble. We also have plenty of scriptural examples of those He did not rescue or took His time rescuing. James wrote, "Brothers, as an example of patience in the face of suffering, take the prophets who spoke in the name of the Lord. As you know, we consider blessed those who have persevered. You have heard of Job's perseverance and have seen what the Lord finally brought about. The Lord is full of compassion and mercy" (James 5:10-11). The word *persevere* means literally to "to remain under" hardship, precisely what none of us wish to do but what God calls us to do. In the noun form the word is often translated "patience." This definition expresses the opposite of our natural response, which is to escape from hardship as soon as possible.

Those in the church who believe in Ryan's healing quote "Jesus Christ is the same yesterday and today and forever" (Heb. 13:8). They reason that Jesus healed when He was on earth, and He has not changed. In addition, they say, God has promised only good things for us. Illness could not be good. Therefore, if we believe, God will keep His word and heal. It has to happen because God keeps His promises.

This view demonstrates immense faith in God's abilities. It also assumes that there is absolutely no good in suffering, except perhaps to give God an opportunity to reveal His power by curing it. And this view assumes that God mends promptly what we want Him to mend. It is a partially scriptural view of suffering. It affirms the absolute power of God, the fact that He loves us, that He answers prayer, that He is consistent.

But the fully scriptural view of suffering is more complex than that. It accommodates both the goodness of God and the reality of the consequences of sin. It includes many promises from God, all of which He keeps faithfully.

We don't want to get into a proof-texting contest about healing. And we do not want to belittle anyone's pain or the sincere, tortured questioning which accompanies any experience of unexplained hurt. Why do human beings suffer? The question is as old as Job. We believe in a good and all-powerful God, and yet we undergo things which it seems a good God would not want us to undergo. All Christians who have ever tried to witness have had the issue thrown at them, and with good reason. It is a part of Christian faith which apparently does not make sense.

And it is this very difficult, legitimate question which Walt and others in the church are avoiding. They have given up asking why Ryan suffers; they have chosen to believe instead that God has promised Ryan will *not* suffer but will recover. Since he and all who love him are quite

87

obviously suffering, they or the church or somebody must be failing to have enough faith in God's promises.

Learning to Persevere through Pain

James opened his letter with words often quoted in an ironic tone: "Consider it pure joy, my brothers, whenever you face trials of many kinds, because you know that the testing of your faith develops perseverance. Perseverance must finish its work so that you may be mature and complete, not lacking anything" (James 1:2-4). There's the word *persevere* again. Phillips' paraphrase is a classic: "When all kinds of trials and temptations crowd into your lives, my brothers, don't resent them as intruders, but welcome them as friends!"

We use James' words both to buck up and to reprimand people who are complaining about their numerous problems. If this Scripture promises anything, it promises that we will have trials as a necessary part of our growth in Christ. It clearly states that trials test our faith. We know that all too well. It also says that as we *endure* the testing of our faith, we develop perseverance which in turn develops maturity in us.

In plainer language, there is something about hanging in there when we're hurting that makes us grow up.

Right away a logical question arises: If enduring a problem for a while makes us grow up, might our growth be stunted if the problem is removed too early?

It's easy to say "Sure!" when the problem is our car that keeps dying at every stop sign or a brief period of being without writing assignments. The problem of a seven-year-old with cancer is in another league. Another league but the same ballpark. It still comes back to the basic question of whether God has promised to remove difficulty in response to the prayer of faith, or if He sometimes chooses to leave us in suffering for His own purposes.

A Scriptural View of Suffering

The Bible teaches us that difficulties are stepping-stones to maturity if and when we surrender them to the Lord and let Him use them for our growth.

Suffering teaches us both that we cannot, and that we can, handle our problems.

Suffering first of all teaches us that we are not all-powerful. In an environment which shouts at us that we are gods, that's a valuable lesson. In order to find out that the message of our omnipotence is false, we have to come to some point where we test our human strength and find ourselves wanting. Suffering accomplishes that for us. For some of us, it takes surprisingly little suffering to bring us to the end of ourselves.

After pain talks us out of our invincibility, it can do something else for us. It makes us reach for God. Again, that's a vital lesson in this culture which tells us we don't need God, if God even exists. We can choose to let pain turn us toward Him.

Perhaps we reach for Him at first through an angry question: "Why did this happen to me?" At least we're talking to Him. Better to tell Him how mad we are at Him than to shut Him out entirely. He can handle our questions and even our anger. Otherwise, He would never have inspired Psalms like 74 and 88.

After teaching us that we can't handle things, in the end suffering teaches us that we *can* handle things when we rely on the Lord's strong help. Psalms 98 and 103 testify to the strength He gives in trouble and His deliverance from trouble.

Pain prods us to give up our self-reliance and rely on Him instead. If we do that, and only if we do that, then eventually we can see the experience as a privilege which helped us know Him better.

Christ's Suffering

Tied up in our problems, we may accuse God of forgetting us or ignoring us or even causing the problem Himself. But we can never accuse Him of standing aloof from pain while He dispenses easy, safe platitudes. He has been through what we go through. He even did it willingly.

Paul wrote that "the message of the cross is foolishness to those who are perishing" (1 Cor. 1:18). If pain has no value, certainly it was "foolish" for God to subject Himself to it. How could anything good could come out of letting mankind crucify Him? "But to us who are being saved it is the power of God. . . . For the foolishness of God is wiser than man's wisdom, and the weakness of God is stronger than man's strength" (1 Cor. 1:18, 25).

"The weakness of God" is what we see on the cross, when God submitted to the worst that we could do to Him. Not because He was a masochist but because through this He could bring us salvation. Love overcame the natural human abhorrence of suffering. Love for the Father and for us made Jesus able to say in Gethsemane, "My Father, if it is possible, may this cup be taken from Me. Yet not as I will, but as You will" (Matt. 26:39).

Through the worst thing that mankind could do to God, God brought the best thing for mankind. If that great fact doesn't redeem suffering in our eyes, we are hopeless pessimists.

Besides the examples in the Gospels, there are other scriptural pictures of the suffering of Christ. Peter, an eye-witness to Christ's ordeal (and nearly a traitor to it) had much reason to meditate on the meaning of Christ's suffering. He wrote:

But if you suffer for doing good and you endure it, this is commendable before God. To this you were called, because Christ suffered for you, leaving you an example, that you should follow in His steps. . . . He entrusted Himself to Him who judges justly. He Himself bore our sins in His body on the tree, so that we might die to sins and live for righteousness; by His wounds you have been healed (1 Peter 2:20-21, 23-24).

If Jesus' suffering carried our sins and healed us, who can call His suffering entirely bad? Who can call any suffering entirely bad if God can bring good out of it?

Later in the same letter Peter reminded his readers not to be amazed when bad things happen to them, even though they are believers.

Dear friends, do not be surprised at the painful trial you are suffering, as though something strange were happening to you. But rejoice that you participate in the sufferings of Christ, so that you may be overjoyed when His glory is revealed. . . . If you suffer as a Christian, do not be ashamed, but praise God that you bear that name (1 Peter 4:12-13, 16).

If you're a Christian, Peter says, expect to get hurt! Who wants to hear that? Nobody. But we can never accuse God of hiding the fact from us or tricking us into thinking everything will be rosy. And we can never accuse God of refusing to take His own medicine.

God is also merciful, and Peter's letter ends in hope that suffering is not going to go on forever: "And the God of all grace, who called you to His eternal glory in Christ, after you have suffered a little while, will Himself restore you and make you strong, firm, and steadfast. To Him be the power for ever and ever. Amen" (1 Peter 5:10-11).

God's Promises

The worst that can happen to us is not going to go on forever. The hurts of this life show us that this life isn't perfect and make us long for something better. The "something better" is not an illusory hope; God promises it to us when He promises us heaven.

John had a vision of the new heaven and new earth, and he heard a voice from God's throne promise, "He will wipe every tear from their eyes. There will be no more death or mourning or crying or pain, for the old order of things has passed away" (Rev. 21:4).

Inadequate as this vision is to relieve the current stabbing pain of a spinal tap or an amputee's "ghost" limbs, it is nevertheless real. It will be ours. Heaven is already a living experience for millions of people who had faith in Jesus, regardless of whether their earthly lives were comfortable or not. It's a certainty for us whether we die physically or the Lord returns while we are still alive. Paul wrote, "I consider that our present sufferings are not worth comparing with the glory that will be revealed in us. . . . the creation itself will be liberated from its bondage to decay and brought into the glorious freedom of the children of God" (Rom. 8:18, 21).

But what about now? What promises are for all believers, here and now, today, in the midst of suffering? Christ has also promised to be with us no matter what happens. One of His parting promises to His disciples was "And surely I will be with you always, to the very end of the age" (Matt. 28:20). It was very important to Him that they know He was not actually leaving them. In coming times they (and we) would have reasons to doubt that He was there. Right after He gave the Great Commission to make disciples of all nations, He assured us that He will never leave us. If we're going to carry His message to a hostile world, we need to know that. When we encounter opposition of any kind—physical, spiritual, emotional—we need to know He is with us.

God may relieve our suffering in response to our prayers of faith—in His own time, for His own purposes. But no matter what He *does*, He *promises* us His presence and the grace to bear up under whatever happens in a way that brings honor to Him.

Are we being negative about God's guarantees of health and well-being when we say we cannot pray in absolute assurance that Ryan will be healed? On the contrary, we believe we are being realistic, even though realism does not always square with what we'd like to see happen.

No one wishes more than we do that Ryan would be healed. We'd like to think of Walt someday watching Ryan, bright-eyed and healthy, play with his spaceship models on the floor. Perhaps by God's grace that scene will happen. Certainly it *can* happen. But—there is no guarantee from God that it *will* happen.

The guarantee is that no matter what happens, Ryan belongs to the Lord, and His grace will be sufficient. Our prayer is that in anything that happens to us, we will believe and live what we write about God's promises.

CHAPTER EIGHT

Life Is Always Fair

The adults of the 1980s, who were young people of the 1960s, often complain that today's young people are passive and apathetic toward the wrongs in society. "Why aren't they out changing things?" their elders ask.

Belief in change gives the sort of gritty optimism which made the civil rights movement possible and which now spurs people to campaign for changes in abortion laws. It gives rise to groups such as MADD and SADD which try to stop drunk driving. It drove people to look for ways to vaccinate against smallpox and polio and all those diseases we barely think about today. Recently, it put the U.S. back in space with the Discovery shuttle.

With all our faith in the changeablity of things, it has begun to seem that anything is possible if enough people try hard enough long enough. Has there ever been a society on earth with so much faith in the fixability of things? When life doesn't work, we are deeply offended. If something is wrong today, we think we need only wait for technology's next step, and we get violently impatient if technology is slow. We're angry that there is still no cure for Alzheimer's disease or AIDS, because there's *got* to be. We were stunned and furious when the Challenger exploded, so accustomed had we become to safe space travel. Life is *repairable*, we think, and if these problems are still with us, somebody isn't on the ball.

Our American demand that "Bad things shouldn't happen" is more than a philosophical statement. It is a *technological* demand which insists that by now somebody should have *done* something about our problems. In fact many suspect they have already been conquered if the government or the military or the doctors or whoever is the keeper of secrets would just release the information to us.

Certainly it's true that space shuttle explosions and debilitating diseases are tragedies. No sane person would say they are desirable or good. We know from the Bible as well as from our own consciences that in God's plan, mankind was not supposed to experience evil. In a philosophical sense it's true that such things "ought not to happen," and we should spare no effort at finding ways to keep tragedies like them from happening.

That's subtly different, however, from the message coming at us from all around, which says that all things are fixable and that with enough effort, everything will be fine and fair. Not someday in heaven but here and now on this earth in this life. If it hasn't happened yet, it's because people aren't doing their job. Then if I complain loudly enough to the right people, I will get what I want and life will start being fair to me.

What Ought to Be
All our inner moral senses tell us life is supposed to be fair. Things ought to work out evenly. Good behavior should be rewarded while bad behavior is punished. There should be

equal justice for everyone. No one should be able to get away with anything or have an unfair advantage. All things should be distributed equally—well, wait a minute, maybe things don't have to be *completely* equitable, but at least no one should be able to get ahead by means unavailable to the rest of us.

Two facts about justice should be obvious right away.

First, there is a great discrepancy between what ought to be and what actually is. Life is manifestly inequitable. Other people do get ahead by means wildly inaccessible to the rest of us. "Bad" people get away with all kinds of things they shouldn't. Terminal diseases, like Ryan's (mentioned in the last chapter), do attack "good" people.

Although many of us are enjoying a time of prosperity, the number of people in the United States without a place to live continues to grow: "The nation's homeless population has risen 25% in the past year, according to the National Coalition for the Homeless" (Amy Wilentz, "Cold Comfort for the Homeless," *Time*, January 18, 1988, p. 22). "'The economic recovery is leaving many poor Americans behind,' said Robert Greenstein of the Center on Budget and Policy Priorities, a private research group. According to Census Bureau statistics, median family income for whites increased from $31,935 to $32,274. For blacks, median family income dipped from $18,247 to $18,098" ("North American Scene," *Christianity Today*, October 21, 1988, p. 38).

On an international scale, we learn of "large-scale killings of civilians by security forces. . . . use of torture by clandestine groups linked to government. . . . return of right-wing "death squads" with military links. . . . large scale starvation as a political weapon" ("Bad Company: A Year of Abuses," *Newsweek*, February 20, 1989, p. 28).

Life isn't just unfair today; it was unfair in biblical times.

When Job's "friends" tried to tell him that God punishes the wicked and exalts the righteous, Job shot back,

> How often is the lamp of the wicked snuffed out? How often does calamity come upon them, the fate God allots in his anger? How often are they like straw before the wind, like chaff swept away by a gale? ... Have you never questioned those who travel? Have you paid no regard to their accounts—that the evil man is spared from the day of calamity, that he is delivered from the day of wrath? (Job 21:17-18, 29-30)

Everyday observation told Job that justice in this life was a myth. Our observation today tells us the same thing. The injustice of life here and now isn't good, but it's a fact. For the sake of our own mental health, we all have to confess that life is not fair.

There is a second obvious fact about justice: that we all cheerfully tolerate injustice as long as it's weighted in our favor.

Right now you are reading this book. Is it fair that very early in life you had the opportunity to learn to read and write while much of the world's population never had that opportunity? Is it fair that we have lived to adulthood while many people, born the same days we were born, died in disease-infested villages with no sanitation?

That's not the kind of injustice that galls us. It's the unfairness weighted against us, or against people and causes we care about, that makes us gnash our teeth and march on Washington and write letters to the editor and circulate petitions.

Right away we see that most of us are unfair about fairness. We want fairness for our side more than we want fairness for the other side.

God's Example of Justice

Is justice something worth working for? Of course it is. The Law, the Prophets, and the Gospels tell us God is a God of justice. Scripture tells us He wants us to treat each other fairly and work for fairness for others. In Deuteronomy 16:18-20, for example, God gave the Israelites instructions for living in the land He would give them:

> Appoint judges and officials for each of your tribes in every town the Lord your God is giving you, and they shall judge the people fairly. Do not pervert justice or show partiality. Do not accept a bribe, for a bribe blinds the eyes of the wise and twists the words of the righteous. Follow justice and justice alone, so that you may live and possess the land the Lord your God is giving you.

Throughout the Old Testament the prophets of God spoke loudly and firmly against the injustices of their time. In one of his nicer pronouncements, Isaiah said, "Woe to those who make unjust laws, to those who issue oppressive decrees, to deprive the poor of their rights and rob my oppressed people of justice, making widows their prey and robbing the fatherless" (Isa. 10:1-2).

Jesus had His own way of working against the unfairness of life. As He began His ministry, He proclaimed Himself the fulfillment of Isaiah's prophecy: "The Spirit of the Lord is on Me, because He has anointed Me to preach good news to the poor. He has sent Me to proclaim freedom for the prisoners and recovery of sight for the blind, to release the oppressed, to proclaim the year of the Lord's favor" (Luke 4:18-19). His liberation was spiritual, but it also involved the physical, as He showed by healing and feeding people as well as teaching. He authorized His disciples to do the same life-changing acts: "When Jesus had called the Twelve together, He gave them power and authority to drive out all demons and to cure diseases and He sent them out to preach the kingdom of God and to heal the sick" (Luke 9:1-2).

God tells us to do something about the injustices which oppress other people. When our efforts are led by His Spirit, we can confidently oppose evil and know that He is with us. We do not have to heave a resigned sigh in the face of injustice and say, "Well, that's just the way it is."

God also tells us to willingly give up the right to justice for ourselves, for His sake. This is something we would rather not find in Scripture. It irritates our nature.

We can't read the Sermon on the Mount without an uncomfortable feeling that Jesus is telling us to make ourselves vulnerable to abuse. "Blessed are the merciful. . . . If someone strikes you on the right cheek, turn to him the other also. And if someone wants to sue you and take your tunic, let him have your cloak as well. . . . Love your enemies and pray for those who persecute you" (Matt. 5:7, 39-40, 44). He also said, "Whoever wants to be first must be slave of all" (Mark 10:44) and, "If anyone wants to follow in my footsteps, he must give up all right to himself, carry his cross every day and keep close behind me" (Luke 9:24, PH).

Christ lived those words. When God became a man, He fought for fairness for others, but He did not demand it for Himself. He willingly submitted to abuse and death for our sake. If we follow in His footsteps, we will do the same for Him and others.

We do not like that. We think we should be able to follow Christ in self-sacrifice while simultaneously getting what we want. Somewhere we have moved away from the idea that "this life is unfair, but that is to be expected because we live in a fallen world." Once, when a loved one became ill and died, it was accepted as part of living in a fallen world but with the hope that even death would be overcome when Christ returned. There were times when this led to an unbiblical fatalism that blindly accepted tragedy as God's will. But now we have come to the very different position of demanding that this life has to be fair because it's my right.

Jeremiah's Response to Unfairness

We are not alone in our complaints: "Why me?" and "It's not fair." Jeremiah also complained to God about unfairness in his life.

> You are always righteous, O Lord, when I bring a case before you. Yet I would speak with you about your justice: Why does the way of the wicked prosper? Why do the faithless live at ease? You have planted them, and they have taken root; they grow and bear fruit. You are always on their lips but far from their hearts. Yet you know me, O Lord; you see me and test my thoughts about you. Drag them off like sheep to be butchered! Set them apart for the day of slaughter! How long will the land lie parched and the grass in every field be withered? Because those who live in it are wicked, the animals and birds have perished. Moreover, the people are saying, "He will not see what happens to us" (Jeremiah 12:1-4).

God's answer must have been unexpected to Jeremiah: "If you have raced with men on foot and they have worn you out, how can you compete with horses? If you stumble in safe country, how will you manage in the thickets by the Jordan?" (12:5) Instead of defending His fairness, God simply agreed that this life is unfair, and it probably will get worse. Jeremiah needed fortitude, not a complaining spirit, to get through what was going to happen to him.

As we look further at the life of Jeremiah, we find that he did not just complain about unfairness in his day. Like all of the other prophets, he took a firm stand against it. Wherever he saw unfairness, he pointed it out and declared God's righteous judgment on it. How often he must have cried out against the unfairness of his own situation. While the false prophets were free to proclaim whatever lie was convenient—winning support from the king—Jeremiah was bound to speak only the truth.

Accepting Unfairness

Many years later, facing death in a Roman prison, the Apostle Paul wrote to Timothy: "Do your best to come to me quickly, for Demas, because he loved this world, has deserted me and has gone to Thessalonica. Crescens has gone to Galatia, and Titus to Dalmatia. Only Luke is with me. . . . At my first defense, no one came to my support, but everyone deserted me. May it not be held against them" (2 Tim. 4:9-11, 16). That part of Paul's letter seems to be filled with the unfairness of this life. Then he turned to the real hope that sustained him:

But the Lord stood at my side and gave me strength, so that through me the message might be fully proclaimed and all the Gentiles might hear it. And I was delivered from the lion's mouth. The Lord will rescue me from every evil attack and will bring me safely to his heavenly kingdom. To him be glory forever and ever. Amen (2 Tim. 4:17-18).

Is there a paradox here? Paul had just finished telling Timothy that "I am already being poured out like a drink offering, and the time has come for my departure. I have fought the good fight, I have finished the race, I have kept the faith. Now there is in store for me the crown of righteousness, which the Lord, the righteous Judge, will award to me on that day" (2 Tim. 4:6-8). He was sure he was going to die, yet he praised God for rescue. He knew that even Satan's final attack would not defeat him, because he would be promoted to the Lord's presence.

Paul did not need to experience fairness in order to rejoice during his life.

We need to accept the fact that unfairness is a fact of this life, knowing that one day all things will be made right. In the meantime, we can acknowledge all the good that is happening to us. We can get our minds off our own hurt by doing what we can to overcome the injustice in the world around us while trusting God who judges all things righteously.

CHAPTER NINE

What Matters Is the Here and Now

We had owned our computer for only a few months when we discovered it was obsolete. Yes. It was already out-of-date, antiquated, superannuated.

"Sorry," said the computer magazines and some of our computer-owning friends. The company isn't even making our model anymore. Our computer is now *too slow.*

Never mind that it can flawlessly type out 100-page manuscripts while we dine by candlelight. Never mind that with our computer's help we can be working on the rough draft of an article at 3 p.m. and get it to the post office by 5 p.m.

Our machine is still fast enough for us and apparently fast enough for the editors who set our deadlines. It's efficient, dependable, and (except for eating Chapter 11 of this book) cooperative. No matter. The fact that faster machines now exist obviously means that we need to catch up.

But are efficiency and speed the ultimate values?

How did efficiency and speed become elevated to such a

position in the first place?

Communication has become instantaneous. There are phones on planes, phones in cars, laptop computers, long-distance beepers. Ask a question now, get a response in seconds. Apparently there is no value in allowing other people time to think before they answer, or in pausing to reflect while we wait for the answer. Our focus is clearly on the here and now.

Even from a purely secular viewpoint, there are dangers in the push-to-do-everything here and now. James Campbell Quick, professor of organizational behavior at the University of Texas at Arlington, has this caution about the ever-present technological wonders which expand the workplace to everyplace: "The risk in being able to work around the clock anywhere in the world is that you'll do just that. You may get a lot done, but you also may be dead sooner" (Ellen Hoffman, "Have Office Will Travel," *Psychology Today*, September 1988, p. 46).

Even in our homes with dishwashers and microwaves and programmed coffee makers, mornings are hectic and evenings are too short. All our laborsaving devices do not appear to have given us any more time.

Caught up in the mechanics of how to do our jobs and how to run our homes more efficiently, we can fail to take time to analyze the basic message being screamed at us in all this strenuous push-to-do-everything right now. The message is that *the here and now is all that matters.*

No Sense of Past or Future

Why is the present elevated to all-important? *Because we have lost the concept of a past from which we can learn or a future which is going somewhere that matters.* Stripped of yesterday and tomorrow, we naturally strain to get all we can from today.

Writer Philip Yancey takes an imaginative look at what a society might look like if it *did not* believe in an afterlife. He calls his imaginary here-and-now society *Acirema* and describes eight of its characteristics:

1. Aciremans value youth above all else. Since for them nothing exists beyond life on earth, only youth can represent hope.

2. Naturally, Aciremans do not value old age, for elderly people offer a distasteful reminder of the end of life.

3. Acirema emphasizes "image" rather than "substance."

4. Acireman religion focuses exclusively on how one fares in the here and now, for there is no reward system after death.

5. Recently, crime has taken a turn toward the grotesquely violent and bizarre. In other primitive societies, citizens grew up with a vague fear of eternal judgment hanging over them, but Aciremans have no such deterrents to deviant behavior.

6. Aciremans spend billions of dollars to maintain elderly bodies on life-support systems while at the same time they strongly encourage the abortion of fetuses. This is not as paradoxical as it seems, for Aciremans believe that human life begins at birth and ends at death.

7. Until recently, Acireman psychologists had to treat their patients' atavistic [primitive] reactions of fear and anger in the face of death. . . . Aciremans are now taught to view "acceptance" as the most mature response to the perfectly natural state of death.

8. Acireman scientists are still working to eliminate the problem of death.

Yancey sardonically sums up his "mythical" world: "Just thinking about such a society gives me the creeps. I sure am glad I live in the good ol' U.S.A., where, as George Gallup assures us, a full 90 percent of the population believe in an afterlife" ("Imagine There's No Heaven," *Christianity Today*, December 12, 1986, p. 72).

People in our culture stand on the narrow plateau of "now" with an empty canyon on either side. They do not believe in the hereafter, and the past has nothing to say to them either. Just as Yancey expresses concern about our isolation from the future, Allan Bloom, in his book *The Closing of The American Mind*, expresses concern about our isolation from the past, specifically the great books of the past. "The failure to read good books both enfeebles the vision and strengthens our most fatal tendency—the belief that the here and now is all there is" (Simon and Schuster, p. 64).

Instant Physical Beauty and Excellence

"Live for here and now because it's all you get" is the message we hear and see—especially see—all around us. Look at glossy fitness magazines and videos. Certainly the people in them are beautiful by our culture's current standard of beauty. They are externally perfect and keep striving to become more perfect. How long will their "perfection" last? Everywhere, we see a nearly frantic idolizing of temporal health, good looks, and strength. Behind its gloss is fear: once we lose our physical power and beauty, life is lost.

Good stewardship of God's gifts includes taking care of the bodies God gave us. We can take legitimate pleasure in our physicality. Through discipline and hard work many of us may excel at some sport. We enjoy skiing the miles of clean, silent, nearly-deserted national forest trails near our home, and hiking those same hilly trails in the summertime. But we're kidding ourselves if we think we can arrest the natural aging process and be strong and healthy forever.

The pressure to excel in the here and now tempts us to take unethical shortcuts. The 1988 Olympics showed us the sorry misuse of steroids for quick results, despite the rules banning their use and despite long-term risks to health. The Olympics symbolize physical excellence and sportsmanship and honest competition. But because steroids promised results right now, their use for the sake of winning came before ethics and fair play and even before physical well-being.

Instant Money

How we handle our money is another area where "live for here and now" thinking is pervasive. How often are we pressured to overextend our credit in order to have things right now, even though we may not be able to pay for them later?

We hear much about the threat of the "greenhouse effect" and how it is partly being caused by destruction of tropical forests to make room for short-term cash crops. The earth's resources are being depleted for immediate profit, with no thought that the destruction is permanent and the effects threatening to all life.

The examples go on. Get-rich-quick plans promise us instant wealth. Recently we received a chain letter guaranteeing us massive riches by getting thousands of people to send us $5. After a few "generations" of the chain letter, we could be millionaires. Arithmetic shows that you will soon run out of people to send the letter to, since in only a few "generations" of a chain letter, you have exceeded the population of the world.

Instant Spirituality

Not only are there get-rich-quick plans, there are even get-spiritual-quick plans. We're offered a singular spiritual experience or an easy-to-follow method to know God. We are promised instant spiritual victory.

Why are we tempted by these get-spiritual-quick plans? Probably because we've absorbed the world's message that nothing good is accomplished by saying no to ourselves. Shortcuts are attractive. We would like to get to the Promised Land without trekking through the wilderness. We may still believe in theory that we grow in holiness through a lifelong process, yet we want everything now.

God's Work in Our Lives

There are no shortcuts to holy living. In contrast to the ever-present message that "life is here and now," the biblical message is long-range to the point of eternity. God is taking His time with our earthly lives, shaping us to be more like Christ. The here and now matters, of course, because this moment is part of God's creation; we have the responsibility to live this moment for Him. But the value of this present moment is in its relation to eternity. God's view is toward forever.

Have you ever wondered why the Bible is such a large book? Reading the whole book in a year is a major project. God could have inspired a small pamphlet or a slender volume. Instead, He chose to preserve lengthy, detailed accounts of the history of the Jewish people and of the early Christian church. The past is important because God was in it and He wants to teach us through it. Referring to the account of the Israelites in the desert, Paul wrote: "Now these things occurred as examples, to keep us from setting our hearts on evil things as they did.... These things happened to them as examples and were written down as warnings for us, on whom the fulfillment of the ages has come" (1 Cor. 10:6, 11).

Just as God teaches us from the past, He also has a purpose for our future. He aims for developing Christlikeness in our character: "And we know that in all things God works for the good of those who love Him, who have been called according to His purpose. For those God foreknew He also predestined to be conformed to the likeness of His Son, that He might be the firstborn among many brothers" (Rom. 8:28-29). God's purpose is to shape us and make us more like Christ. He does not appear to be in a hurry about it. He is working on the molding of our inner lives, something which is not achieved instantly.

But we chafe under God's timing. We live here and now, and we want here and now to be fun. If it isn't, we tend to feel cheated.

But if we know God, we see beyond any discomforts of now, thanking God for what He has done in the past and trusting Him for what He is going to accomplish in us.

When we're tempted to think this process is taking too much time in the here and now, we can know we're in good company. Hebrews 11, the "faith" chapter, mentions numerous Old Testament saints who died in faith, still looking ahead to God's promises. Though some of these saints might have felt their lives were wasted because they did not immediately receive what they believed was coming, God still counted them faithful and their lives valuable. The writer of Hebrews mentions Abel, Enoch, Noah, Abraham, Isaac, and Jacob: "All these people were still living by faith when they died. They did not receive the things promised; they only saw them and welcomed them from a distance. . . . they were longing for a better country—a heavenly one. Therefore God is not ashamed to be called their God, for he has prepared a city for them. . . . These were all commended for their faith, yet none of them received what had been promised. God had planned something better for us so that only together with us would they be made perfect" (Heb. 11:13, 16, 39-40).

Just beyond the "faith" chapter of Hebrews is the "discipline" chapter. If we judge the value of God's loving chastening purely on how it might feel in the here and now, we will resist it and reject it. God's loving purpose will be misinterpreted, and He will not have that opportunity to do His work in us. "God disciplines us for our good, that we may share in His holiness. No discipline seems pleasant at the time, but painful. Later on, however, it produces a harvest of righteousness and peace for those who have been trained by it" (Heb. 12:10-11).

Eternal Joy with God

God's shaping of our earthly lives is only the beginning of the process. Heaven is real, and one value of our earthly trials is that they prepare us for eternal joy with God. Looking forward to being raised with Christ, Paul wrote, "Therefore we do not lose heart. Though outwardly we are wasting away, yet inwardly we are being renewed day by day. For our light and momentary troubles are achieving for us an eternal glory that far outweighs them all. So we fix our eyes not on what is seen, but on what is unseen. For what is seen is temporary, but what is unseen is eternal" (2 Cor. 4:16-18).

Christ did not take an easy shortcut to our salvation. He endured the cross for the joy of doing God's will. If His sight had been purely on the here and now of that time, what would have been the value of undergoing such a painful and unjust death? And where would our salvation be now? But His sight was on the future, which gave Him the courage to deny Himself in the present. Therefore "Let us fix our eyes on Jesus, the author and perfecter of our faith, who for the joy set before him endured the cross, scorning its shame, and sat down at the right hand of the throne of God" (Heb. 12:2).

If we have confidence in God, who is the God of the future, we can obey James 5:7: "Be patient, then, brothers, until the Lord's coming." Christ will come again. He is not yet here in the glory of His second advent, though He is here in His Spirit. As we wait for Him to return, we learn (as we learn while waiting for any of God's promises) that "Faith is being sure of what we hope for and certain of what we do not see" (Heb. 11:1) and that God's grace is sufficient for us. Knowing His reliability in the past, trusting His faithfulness in the future, we can confidently live for *Him* in the here and now.

MESSAGE FOUR:

You Can Write Your Own Rules.

We cherish our freedom. Freedom is what we think of first when we think of being American. Because freedom is such a good and laudable thing, it's particularly dangerous when made into an idol.

We're offered innumerable choices and told to act boldly as free agents. To give up a freedom is considered a weakness. Yet problems continually come up when our liberties conflict with other people's liberties.

Commitment necessarily means giving up freedom— whether it's commitment to God, another person, the church, or a cause. In Christ we can be loosed from our bondage to personal freedom and find true freedom to be ourselves in serving Him and others.

CHAPTER TEN

Freedom Is Everything

Mark, our former neighbor, was addicted to personal freedom.

He loved to hunt and fish, but he considered fishing licenses and hunting licenses to be ridiculous red tape. He bragged, "Nobody in my family ever bought a license, and I'm not going to either."

One day the game warden met him in the woods. Mark had some trouble explaining what he was doing out there with a gun and several deceased grouse, so he got a heavy fine. There were already fines on his head for various driving violations. He couldn't afford all his fines, and anyway he thought they were unfair, so he didn't pay them. With thousands of dollars of unpaid fines hanging over his head, Mark was always in danger of doing time in the county jail.

A few licenses would have been a lot cheaper than all those fines. With a license in his pocket, Mark could have hunted and fished in freedom, without having to watch for the warden. With a valid driver's license in his wallet and some respect for traffic laws, he wouldn't have had to stay on the lookout for the squad car. But there was something about the seductive appeal of freedom that made Mark take those risks. Doing what he pleased at the moment was worth everything, even the danger of losing large amounts of money and perhaps even his physical liberty for a time.

Mark's freedom had a price, however. His wife, Laura, eventually had enough and told him to leave. (They were legally married; surprisingly, Mark had consented to a marriage license.) He began living with another girl but sometimes came to see Laura. She filed for divorce; he talked of contesting it. She found it hard to resist letting him in when he came to the door, but she told him she didn't want him coming around while he was living with someone else.

"Make up your mind—is it going to be me or her?" she demanded.

One night Mark asked, only half jokingly, "Why can't I have two wives?"

Well, why couldn't he? According to Mark's standards, that would have been fine. Both women gave him pleasure in different ways. In his own way he would have said he loved them both. Freedom dictated that nothing should restrain him. So why not alternate between two women? One would give the security of a legal relationship, the other would give the excitement of something different on the side, and everybody would be happy.

But there were occasional glimpses of another side to Mark. The divorce papers were delivered to him at his workplace. His coworker told Laura, "When those papers came, Mark went into the other room and cried."

Freedom is a cruel master. Mark insisted on writing his own rules for life. Solitary rule making might work fine on a desert island but not in a society among other people who write opposite rules. Mark clashed with others and came out the loser.

He grew up believing a prevailing message of our culture: "You have to do what makes you happy, and happiness is a state of being free to do as you choose, unhindered by anybody else's rules or opinions."

Believing this message means that happiness becomes dependent on making choices without interference from others and without concern as to how those choices will affect others. In living reality, those conditions almost never exist, and Mark is doomed to be frustrated by his inability to be totally free.

The Bondage of Freedom

As a master, freedom is possessive and deceptive. It tells us we *have* to do what we want. Freedom insists that my own immediate wants must come first. Morality, love, conscience, legality, tradition, church, God—all that might possibly be a good external influence on me—are sacrificed to personal autonomy.

We knew a young person who chronically skipped school. His parents put him in the small Christian school where Dale was teaching literature and composition. The boy still played hookey and refused to do assignments. His parents did not support the school's insistence that he be there and do the work. Eventually he had to leave the school. He went back to public school, sporadically. He is too young to drive but drives anyway without a license or permit. He just doesn't like anybody telling him what to do. Is his free-spirited life exciting? Hardly. He hangs around a local gas station/snack bar drinking coffee and talking about how he hopes the police don't catch him driving. Sometimes he comes to visit Dale, but he doesn't have much to talk about. He is extremely bored.

Freedom dictates that every person must act as a law unto himself. The result is not inner liberty; it is bondage to the boredom of listening only to ourselves. It's far from what Jesus promised in John 10:10: "I have come that they may have life, and have it to the full." Instead, it's more like the chaos in Israel at the end of the book of Judges, when "every man did that which was right in his own eyes" (Judges 21:25, KJV).

Yet personal autonomy reigns in our culture in spite of its poor record in our inner lives. It has become our new absolute standard for behavior. We measure the advisability or inadvisability of an action by whether it will leave us still free to do as we please. In only a few decades, the dominant standard of right and wrong in our culture has switched from the Bible to each individual's personal desire and preference. Of course not everyone in this country used to follow the Bible faithfully, but at least most people would have acknowledged the Bible as the ultimate guide to morality, whether they lived by it or not. Now, individual freedom is the accepted ultimate guide for behavior. To resort to any external standard for values is considered a sign of weakness or immaturity.

Sensing Right and Wrong

Still, hard as we try, we can't get away from right and wrong. Paul wrote that the Gentiles who didn't have God's written law still "show that the requirements of the law are written on their hearts, their consciences also bearing witness, and their thoughts now accusing, now even defending them" (Rom. 2:15).

Sometimes when people are trying hardest to deny the existence of right and wrong, their very language betrays them. The results can be amusing.

Remember Les, the atheist, from chapter 5? The one who wanted to discuss the supposed contradictions in Jewish dietary laws in Leviticus and Deuteronomy? We did go to see him in his book-lined apartment, bringing dinner with us. He never mentioned the dietary laws in the Bible, but we talked about almost everything else.

Les explained his ideas. We explained our ideas. Both sides were a combination of intellect and emotion. We all drank a lot of tea. Neither of us convinced the other. Les was insistent that there cannot be any right and wrong, any good and bad, any moral law, or any objective truth because there is no God ("no Law-Giver," as he put it) to define those things. We have our truth, he has his truth, and it's all equally true, he kept saying.

That is, he said everything was equally true until either of the two of us mentioned God. Then he met everything we said with phrases like "You're wrong!" "That's not true!" "Absolutely false!" and so forth.

Sandy's junior highers laughed when she told them the story. "He's not very consistent," they pointed out.

Much as people like Les want to say that everyone's ideas of reality are equally valid, they find it impossible to keep value judgments out of their language. They want to tell you that they're right and you're wrong even though, to be consistent, they should accept your point as perfectly valid for you. They are using the very concepts they reject.

Les, the atheist who can't get away from God, also can't get away from right and wrong. It's written on his being. It creeps into his language no matter how hard he tries to stifle it.

The Illusion of Total Freedom

There's slavery in making our own rules. Les is not even free to consider the possibility of the existence of God. He would threaten his personal freedom too much. Whenever God is mentioned, Les must instantly go on the defensive. There's too much at stake.

None of us like to be confined. We feel threatened by rules which may restrict our freedom. Yet, in our normal, everyday lives, we all see the value of some kind of rules. A smoothly running society would be impossible without at least a minimal set of mutually-agreed-on standards for behavior. Rules are by definition restrictive. They have to be.

Traffic laws are confining. Total freedom in traffic would be to have no speed limits, no stoplights, no center lines, no lanes, and no "No Parking" signs. That would be fine for driving in the Sahara Desert. It might work almost as well in the Bonneville Salt Flats. But in normally populated areas, the result would be a nationwide traffic jam. Eventually, only the daring or the suicidal would feel free to drive at all because driving would be too dangerous.

Total freedom is an illusion. We continually come up against other people's wills, circumstances, our own human limitations, the shortness of life, and countless other restrictions we can't do anything about.

Then do we have free will? Of course we do. God gives us the free moral will to choose between right and wrong; however, the choice is only that—between right and wrong. There is no third alternative of independent individuality. Scripture says that total autonomy is an illusion. Our freedom lies in choosing the right, which is to know God and to do His will.

No Free Agents

We think of slavery as a very bad thing. Yet Paul wrote that in a sense we all must be slaves to something. "Don't you know that when you offer yourselves to someone to obey him as slaves, you are slaves to the one whom you obey— whether you are slaves to sin, which leads to death, or to obedience, which leads to righteousness?" (Rom. 6:16)

We might respond, "Well then, we won't offer ourselves

to anyone! We'll be free agents! After all, isn't this the land of the free and the home of the brave?" But the choice of total personal freedom is not available to us. There are only two choices: follow God or follow sin. Opting for personal independence is actually a choice for sin because it is a choice against God.

Centuries ago God offered the Israelites only two options: "This day I call heaven and earth as witnesses against you that I have set before you life and death, blessings and curses. Now choose life. . . . for the Lord is your life" (Deut. 30:19-20). There were two ways the people could go, and God was honest with them about which way would be best. Through their long history, the Israelites sometimes chose foolishly and sometimes wisely, but they always chose either death or life. A quick survey of the church's history and our personal histories reveals that we too are always choosing either life or death.

God asks us to become slaves to Himself, not so He can oppress us but so He can set us free. We imagine we keep ourselves "free" by avoiding His lordship, but such "freedom" is no freedom at all. It is slavery to sin, which leads to spiritual death. Paul urges us to become slaves of God instead:

> Just as you used to offer the parts of your body in slavery to impurity and to ever-increasing wickedness, so now offer them in slavery to righteousness leading to holiness. When you were slaves to sin, you were free from the control of righteousness. What benefit did you reap at that time from the things you are now ashamed of? Those things result in death! But now that you have been set free from sin and have become slaves to God, the benefit you reap leads to holiness, and the result is eternal life (Rom. 6:19-22).

True Freedom

We carry many images of freedom in our heads. The word may make us picture eagles soaring unhindered above vast canyons. No fences, state troopers, or "Keep Out" signs in sight! However, even the eagle in its flight must obey certain laws of aerodynamics. If it folds its wings, it will plummet to earth and die. The river in the depths of the canyon flows where gravity takes it. The rocks have yielded to erosion at varying rates according to their physical composition. There is consistency in how the physical world operates. God created it that way. A world in which those physical laws were random would be a world where eagles could not fly safely at all.

In the same way, a world where moral law is declared inoperative is a world where mankind cannot live safely. We can't even live safely with ourselves, let alone each other, without the structure of God's laws.

Look at the Ten Commandments in Exodus 20:1-17. What kind of society would we have if everyone lived by these laws? It would be a world where God was honored and where human beings were treated with respect and kindness. Good relationships would be primary—our relationship with God and our relationships with each other. Our world would be a good place to live.

We'll never experience a world in which everyone lives by the Ten Commandments—at least not until Christ returns. But God's laws are alive in every heart which has allowed Christ to enter. God foretold the new covenant through the prophet Jeremiah: "I will put my law in their minds and write it on their hearts. I will be their God, and they will be my people. . . . For I will forgive their wickedness and will remember their sins no more" (Jer. 31:33-34)

Speaking of his own freedom, Paul wrote, "Therefore, there is now no condemnation for those who are in Christ

Jesus, because through Christ Jesus the law of the Spirit of life set me free from the law of sin and death" (Rom. 8:1). With the help of the Holy Spirit, and the law of God now written on our hearts, we are now able to follow Martin Luther's advice to "love God and do as you please." True freedom is only found in willing obedience to God's moral law.

It comes down to this question: who has the right to be in control of the universe? Our natural answer is "Me!" God's answer is also "Me!" Whose voice will we obey?

We settle that question, in a way, when we first come to Christ. We admit we've rebelled against God, and we accept His forgiveness, acknowledging that He is Lord. And every day after that, as long as we live, we must reaffirm those facts—not to keep ourselves saved, for His grace does that, but to keep ourselves dependent on Him. It takes a daily act of the will, a daily taking up of the cross (Luke 9:23) to do that.

But it is still possible, with His help, to daily live in true freedom by submitting to His will. Then "you will know the truth, and the truth will set you free. . . . So if the Son sets you free, you will be free indeed" (John 8:32, 36).

CHAPTER ELEVEN

Don't Let Commitment Cramp Your Style

The local hospital chaplain was leading a seminar on "Spiritual Distress." Most of the participants were nurses and other health workers; Sandy was one of the few people there who was not a health professional. The nurses, therapists, and doctors were gathered at the seminar because they were becoming more aware that illness made their patients ask emotional questions about God, life's meaning, and their own mortality. The health workers wanted to be able to help minister to their patients' spirits as well as their bodies.

The chaplain, a former priest now married, was talking about the need for mutual vulnerability in close relationships, particularly in marriage. He posed a hypothetical situation. "Say a woman has $1,200 in a bank account before she gets married," he said. "When she gets married, do you think she should tell her husband about that money?"

Going on years of practical experience in a marriage based on sharing, Sandy's first thought was *Of course. It belongs to both of them now, and the two of them need to decide what they're going to do with it.* She was shocked at the reaction of the group (mostly women). "No way!' nearly all of them said immediately. "That's *her* money! Why does he need to know anything about it? It's none of his business! She'll need that money if she decides to leave him!"

Sandy was a little startled to hear the vehement protectiveness behind the women's words. Would they have been as vehement if the situation were turned around and the husband had the hidden money? Maybe. One thing was obvious: they believed that marriage does *not* require a commitment either to honesty or to the sharing of possessions.

We could argue back and forth all day about how couples should handle their finances. The point here is not the $1,200 but the angry mood of marital self-protectiveness running rampant in that room. No matter how you feel about the mythical bank account, you can't help but wonder how many other secrets these women were keeping from their husbands. And how many bank accounts and other things their husbands were keeping from their wives.

The Anti-marriage Message
"You're having an anniversary? How many years?"

"Eighteen."

"Eighteen years? Eighteen?" That's how our new neighbor reacted when we told her about our anniversary. You'd have thought we claimed to have reached the South Pole and climbed Everest in the same year. We hadn't thought of our staying married for eighteen years as a great accomplishment, but to her—married briefly once, with children fathered by two other men—it was a wondrous feat.

There had been a similar reaction on our anniversary the year before from a single man never married. "Seventeen *years?* I can't imagine staying married for one day!"

People's amazed comments about our long-term marriage would be funny if they didn't betray several disturbing assumptions: (1) any marriage will probably be short-lived, and (2) you're extremely lucky if your marriage endures more than a few years because everybody knows the odds are against you.

We enjoy being odd when it comes to having a long-term marriage. But we're assaulted by an anti-marriage message all the time. If it even gets to us once in a while, what does it do to teenagers or to single people of any age? The message shouts, "Don't get into this; it'll trap you!" What does it do to couples who find themselves experiencing the first taste of disillusionment with each other? The message proclaims, "Bail out! Find somebody else who can make you happy, or go it on your own! Don't think about how much it might hurt the other person."

The divorce rate, the prevalence of couples living together unmarried, and the acceptance of having children out of wedlock all join in a chorused message, and it's a loud one: "Commitment is a trap. It's OK if you can handle it, but most people can't. So who needs it?"

Committed to Freedom

Good marriages are hard work, and the best marriages take the most concentration and commitment. They take energy which is necessarily drained away from other commitments. If people are not willing to make such a radical commitment, perhaps they should consider whether they ought to marry at all, at least right now.

"If you dislike him so much, why did you ever marry him?" we asked a girl in her early twenties who was thinking of divorce after only eighteen months of marriage.

"It was what I wanted last year," she said. "Now it isn't."

She was living with her husband, but she had all her things packed in boxes, ready to move out at a moment's notice. Her commitment, if it was ever there, was long ago packed in one of those moving crates ready to go out the door. True, it would have taken a high level of commitment from anybody to live with her husband. He was at best hard to get along with. But she had decided very early to stop trying.

Our culture's lack of commitment is tied up with the worship of freedom, which we discussed in the last chapter. We are committed, but only to being free. If a current relationship fails to give us what we want, we have every right to abandon ship and look for somebody else who is more likely to make us happy. We feel free to do that because our own freedom and happiness must come first.

A striking black-and-white magazine ad for a CD player shows a young father cuddling a baby. Earphones plugged into Dad's ears lead to a box that's as big as the baby, and the copy assures us: "Quality time. Your moments together are too precious to waste. That's why [this company] created [this particular] CD player" (*Newsweek*, September 5, 1988, pp. 26–27). In other words, your children deserve your undivided time and attention, but while you're giving it to them, you don't have to miss your favorite music.

You've probably had the experience of working on a project with other people, in church, on your job, or in the community, and feeling very committed to it. You naturally like to think that the other people are as committed as you are. Maybe you've been confused and disillusioned to find out, when they suddenly withdraw or lose interest, that they don't care as much as you do. Your first response may be "I'll never commit myself to anything like this again," or "I'll never work with anyone else again." But you'll be the loser. Risky as commitment is, it's riskier to cut yourself off from commitment or cooperation. You'll cheat yourself of many opportunities for fellowship and accomplishment—and for learning how to deal with people!

We once did an original play with several young people. Much as we loved them, they drove us crazy with their haphazard scheduling. Some thought nothing of skipping rehearsals when something more interesting came up. Their response when we complained was very revealing: "Don't worry, I can handle it." The students were not bothered at all by the chaos that their absence caused for the other actors, who had to say their lines to empty spaces.

As we got close to performance, we discovered that several students had committed themselves to being in the play *and* performing at music contests or concerts simultaneously. The same day, the same hour. Again their response was interesting: "You'll have to work something out because if I don't play in that contest I'll get an F." They did the play, but several music directors will probably never speak to us again.

Perhaps it's unfair to entirely blame the kids, who, despite the teachings of their churches, have grown up in a culture whose dominant message is "Do what makes you comfortable." They were obeying the pull of their own individuality. Their commitment was to self, which they've been told all their lives is supposed to come first.

There's a lot to be said for encouraging kids, and adults, to express independent thinking and their own individuality, but something is wrong when individuality completely supplants commitment and when commitment to others means nothing.

Anti-commitment in Business
The anti-commitment message is evident in other places besides marriage and youth. It's changing the world of

business as well. Mitchell Lee Marks, in "The Disappearing Company Man," writes: "In today's lean and mean companies, the new breed of workers, professionals, and executives has shed the traditional gray flannel suits and put on their personal running shoes. They are not company men or women but entrepreneurs whose business is themselves."

Marks goes on to point out that it is not just the employees, mostly middle management, who have changed the way they look at their employers; the companies they work for have also changed, dumping unneeded managers mercilessly without regard for long-term service and loyalty. Marks says, "These shake-ups reflect a major change in what organizational psychologists call the 'psychological contract' between employers and employee. . . . This [former] psychological contract committed both sides to maintaining the relationship, with the employees supplying loyalty and the company steady employment." Now both employees and employers are out for themselves, and it's every man/woman for himself/herself.

In the face of fierce international competition, rapidly changing technology, and the threat of corporate takeovers, today's companies are driven more by short-term profits than long-term growth. This has led to more concern for a worker's immediate performance than long-term loyalty. "The changing psychological contract is driving the business world toward an individualistic work force—men and women who place their trust not in giant corporations but in their own capabilities, self-entrepreneurs who run their careers like privately held corporations" (*Psychology Today*, September 1988, pp. 34–39).

Loving God and Others
A Pharisee tested Jesus by asking him to identify the greatest commandment in the Law. "Jesus replied: 'Love the

Lord your God with all your heart and with all your soul and with all your mind.' This is the first and greatest commandment. And the second is like it: 'Love your neighbor as yourself'" (Matt. 22:37-39). Asked only for the greatest commandment, Jesus replied with the greatest and the second greatest. They are inseparable. "For anyone who does not love his brother, whom he has seen, cannot love God, whom he has not seen" (1 John 4:20). God designed us so that we find our meaning in loving the people He puts us with, as well as loving Him. Sometimes we choose those other people and sometimes they are the last ones we would choose, but we are happiest when we extend His love to them.

Love—for both God and others—is more than a feeling. In fact, our natural feelings can get in the way of love. We may feel warm affection and comradeship for people who think the way we think, but we can do that without loving them with God's love. Showing God's love takes a commitment to whatever is best for the other person no matter how it makes us feel.

It is that kind of commitment which people flee because it might not make them feel good at the moment. Commitment will restrict the absolute freedom which so many people see as the meaning of life. Here again, as in the last chapter, we can see how the tyranny of freedom cuts us off from being who God meant us to be.

Our eighteen plus years together have not always been a picnic. After all, there is more to life than picnics. But we were committed to each other from the start. We believe it is that commitment, rather than chance or personalities or luck or good fortune or even romance, which has kept us together.

That is the very commitment which the message all around us tells us we are foolish to make. Lifelong commitment to anyone or anything is a foreign idea, a frightening idea, to a society of isolated individualists putting their own freedom first. "I think of marriage as a concentration camp," one woman said to the man who wanted to marry her. Fortunately, they didn't get married.

Absolute Commitment to God

The clear message of our culture is that commitment (except to ourselves) isn't worth it.

What do we do, then, with the words of Proverbs: "Trust in the Lord with all your heart and lean not on your own understanding; in all your ways acknowledge Him, and He will make your paths straight" (Prov. 3:5-6)?

Or the words of Peter: "Humble yourselves, therefore, under God's mighty hand, that He may lift you up in due time. Cast all your anxiety on Him because He cares for you" (1 Peter 5:6-7)?

Or the words of Jesus: "Come to me, all you who are weary and burdened, and I will give you rest. Take my yoke upon you and learn from me, for I am gentle and humble in heart, and you will find rest for your souls" (Matt. 11:28-29)?

The Scriptures unapologetically call us to make an absolute commitment to the Lord. He says we cannot live full lives without it. He says our making a commitment to Him, or not making it, determines our eternal destiny.

When we make the commitment of marriage, we count on having love, pleasure, contentment, and a secure relationship. But we cannot make the commitment of marriage without also risking widowhood, rejection, illness, disability, and, at the very least, disruption of our lifelong habits. We do not know what is around the corner.

When we commit ourselves to the Lord, we count on salvation, hope, guidance, peace, and inner-strengthening.

With the package comes danger. Jesus obeyed His Father perfectly, and He wound up being crucified!

Christ said, "Whoever serves me must follow me; and where I am, my servant also will be" (John 12:26). The Lord leads His followers into some dangerous places. Missionaries to remote places face physical danger; Christians who reach out to their neighbors face ridicule, rejection, and misunderstanding.

Commitment takes bravery. We are falsely told that the bravest and noblest people are those who venture out on their own, trusting nothing but themselves. Yet there is no risk of rejection or failed love in such a life of isolation.

Still, Jesus promises, "My Father will honor the one who serves Me" (John 12:26). He says, "Everyone who has left houses or brothers or sisters or father or mother or children or fields for my sake will receive a hundred times as much and will inherit eternal life" (Matt. 19:29).

"If God is for us, who can be against us? . . . Who shall separate us from the love of Christ?" (Rom. 8:31, 35). Commitment to Him, risky as it is, will be rewarded with the gift of His own love. That's how Paul, the former famous Pharisee, could write, "Whatever was to my profit I now consider loss for the sake of Christ. What is more, I consider everything a loss compared to the surpassing greatness of knowing Christ Jesus my Lord, for whose sake I have lost all things. I consider them rubbish, that I may gain Christ" (Phil. 3:7-8). That's what makes being a Christian worth everything.

CHAPTER TWELVE

Responding to the Messages: Proclaiming Truth in a Pluralistic Society

Mandy has left her husband, Cal. We sometimes run into her downtown, but when we ask where she's living or what her phone number is, she changes the subject. Cal has been depressed since Mandy left.

We're planning an informal potluck at our home, and Mandy is avoiding us, so we're inviting Cal.

A few days before the potluck we run into Lenny, an acquaintance we've met a few times. He tells us he's recently broken up with his wife, whom we don't know. We invite Lenny to the get-together also; maybe the two abandoned husbands can console each other, and Lenny looks like he could use a good meal.

The day of the potluck, out of the blue, Mandy calls. "What time is that party tonight? Lenny couldn't remember, and I'm coming as his date. By the way, here's my phone number." Her phone number is the same as Lenny's.

We do a slow panic. What do you say when estranged husband, unfaithful wife, and unfaithful wife's live-in boyfriend all show up with their casseroles at your front door at the same time? "Hi, I think you all know each other"?

Only Lenny's stalled car stops the evening from being a fiasco. Perhaps an angel removed a couple of spark plugs.

If all your acquaintances sing in the church choir and teach Sunday school, you will probably never have problems like this. But the minute you step outside the church circle and bring the world into your life and home, this is the kind of thing that happens.

After the potluck, we weighed the future implications of what almost happened. Would Lenny and Mandy be welcome in our home as a couple even though we believe they're living in sin and hurting our friend Cal? If we don't stay in contact with them, how will they know we still accept them? *Do* we accept them? Now Cal has his own girlfriend and knows about Lenny. He says, "I'm glad Mandy has somebody else." Does he mean it? Should he mean it? Is everything really OK now that everyone's happy? And is any of this our business?

When we first moved here, our time was taken up working in the confines of our home office or the library and going to church functions. Our town is pleasant but not very aggressive about welcoming strangers. We knew no one here. We realized that if we were going to meet anyone outside of church, we would have to go out and make our own society. We did, and situations like Lenny-Mandy-Cal have been happening ever since. In fact, they're increasing. We constantly ask, "How do we accept the sinners without accepting the sin?" God does it all the time. Somehow by His help we must follow His example.

Accepting Sinners

Years ago we started having potlucks like the one mentioned above, inviting all different kinds of people who didn't know each other. If our memory is right, we started the custom when we were living on nearly no income. Everyone would bring food, but no one would want to take any of it home. So we'd live for several days on the leftovers. In all the places we've lived, we've continued the practice even when the refrigerator wasn't bare, hosting Halloween caramel-apple parties, Christmas open houses, Labor Day picnics, and miscellaneous potlucks for no special occasion at all.

Right now we're making plans for Thanksgiving. With no family nearby, we like to invite others who are also at loose ends on holidays. Sometimes we have a "progressive" Thanksgiving, going from house to house: appetizers at one place, salad at the next, turkey at the next (the largest) place, dessert at the last home. It's great. The collection of turkey-eaters at these occasions is usually very interesting—people with not much in common except a desire to enjoy a holiday with other people.

Many of these people believe and live by the false messages we've talked about in this book: that they should be able to have everything, that they have ultimate power within them, that their lives should be problem-free, that they can write their own rules for life. Their attitude toward our Christian faith is one of cheerful tolerance, in some cases respect. They eat their turkey and go away feeling good.

And we ask ourselves: Do they go away changed? Should they? Certainly by knowing us they should see something of Christ and be confronted with whether or not they want to know more.

In all the contacts our diverse interests give us—through church, teaching, theatre, writing, fishing, camping, and varied community activities—we are continually challenged by Paul's words: "So from now on we regard no one from a worldly point of view. . . . God . . . reconciled us to

Himself through Christ and gave us the ministry of reconciliation.... We are therefore Christ's ambassadors, as
though God were making His appeal through us" (2 Cor.
5:16, 18, 20).

Paul's vision of our role as Christ's representatives is
lofty—and frightening. Lofty because God Himself can
speak through us to reach other people. Frightening because any appeal can be rejected. Nobody likes to be rejected. We tell ourselves that they are rejecting Christ and
not us. But if they withdraw from us socially because they
don't want to talk about Christ, we still lose the friendship.

Most of the people in our church are related. To each
other, that is. So our Christian friends are very busy with
family responsibilities and concerns. They have their many
uncles, aunts, cousins, brothers, sisters, and grandparents
to keep track of and look in on. We find our stronger
relationships among the people we've gone out and met,
here and there, however it happened. Without them we
would feel isolated.

Yet, it's just those people to whom the Lord asks us to
minister reconciliation. If we're going to tell them that God
wants to be reconciled with them, we must also tell them
they are separated from God. Some of them don't want to
hear that very much. Most of them don't want to hear that
at all. Will we risk their rejection to say what should be
said?

Sometimes the opportunity comes out of the blue, and
we don't have time to think about the risk. Once Sandy was
acting in a play. While two other actors had a conversation
in a restaurant, she and another actor were supposed to
"meet" at another table and fake a conversation in the
background. Tim was whispering things to her like "What's
your sign?"

She said, "I don't believe in that," and with hardly a

thought she added, "What are your beliefs?"

"About what?"

"I don't know. Life. God. Reality."

Tim proceeded to tell her—right on stage, in a whisper— his beliefs about God, Jesus Christ, life after death, morality, and the Bible. Sandy was also able to tell Tim what she believed, listening to the other actors with one ear so she wouldn't miss her cue for the next scene!

Witnessing of Our Faith

At times like that we don't have time to be scared. We share naturally out of our hearts. Other times we're asleep at the wheel. Through our weaknesses, in unexpected ways, God works through us to proclaim His truth to people.

Can we proclaim that truth unless we're convinced it's true? Of course not. We believe that God has spoken. We are convinced that He wants us to carry His message to others. And our witness comes straight up against the indignation of our culture. The message all around us is that we have no right to tell anyone else what's true. It's up to each person to find his or her own truth. We Christians are free to believe as we wish, but we are intolerant (the ultimate sin) if we suggest that anyone else should believe as we do. There is no absolute truth—except, of course, the absolute truth that no one has the right to tell anyone else what's true. That "truth" is sacred!

Jeremiah, Ezekiel, Isaiah, and Paul would have laughed at that argument. But then we are not Jeremiah, Ezekiel, Isaiah, or Paul. And didn't they all pay a price for their boldness?

In order to have any credible witness to the world, we have to disbelieve our culture's self-righteous proclamation that says we have no right to say anything. We have to believe that God has spoken through Jesus Christ, "the one and only Son, who came from the Father, full of grace and truth" (John 1:14).

How do we witness in this pluralistic society which tells us its pluralism is sacred?

There are at least three things we must do.

1. *We have to listen.* We don't have to believe everything people say, of course, but we do have to know what they're saying in order to be able to talk with them. We have to know what they're *really* saying under the superficial small talk.

All through this book we've quoted people laying bare their beliefs, their values, and their worldview. In order to quote those things, we had to listen. And we had to know what to listen *for.* People don't utter telling statements every time they open their mouths. We have not bothered to quote all the times our friends and neighbors have said, "Cold today, isn't it?" or "Can I borrow a lasagna pan?" We've trained ourselves, in our listening, to identify the words people say which reveal how they look at the world.

The most lasting lesson Sandy gained from her college philosophy class was not the overview of the great philosophers of history, valuable as that was; it was the idea that *what people say and do comes from their basic presuppositions about life.* Once we know what people believe about existence, we can talk with them about existence. Until then, we are only talking about superficialities. For example, we may debate "When does life begin?" which is a technical issue of chronology. The more basic and vital question is "What is the value of human life?" We can argue about "Should there be prayer in public schools?" but the more basic question is "Does belief in God have a place in an educational system which claims to accommodate all views of reality without judging?"

If we listen, people will reveal to us their presuppositions about life. They probably won't lay them out for us in one-two-three order, for they probably are not aware themselves of what their presuppositions are. That's why we have to listen.

Often, the simple statement "I don't understand" can be helpful in witnessing situations. It shows we are willing to listen to the other side, refuting the stereotype that evangelical Christians are narrow-minded, ignorant bigots. The statement also defuses the other person's defensiveness by its honest stance of humility and openness. And it gives the other person a chance to carry his own ideas out to their logical conclusion—and often to talk himself into a corner, like Les, the atheist who said all ideas are equally true and then jumped on us with "You're wrong!" When we countered with "I don't understand," Les had to do a flying change of subject to get himself out of his bind. Given a chance to talk, non-Christians will often talk themselves into such contradictions.

2. *We have to know what we believe.* Once we've listened to people and determined what they believe, we must have a positive response, leading to an aggressive witness for scriptural truth. Otherwise, we're only another individualistic voice in the pluralistic sea, benignly answering, "That's interesting." We are in spiritual warfare, and we have to have on "the full armor of God" which includes "the belt of truth . . . the breastplate of righteousness . . . feet fitted with the readiness that comes from the Gospel of peace . . . the shield of faith . . . the helmet of salvation . . . the sword of the Spirit" (Eph. 6:13-17).

For though we live in the world, we do not wage war as the world does. The weapons we fight with are not the weapons of the world. On the contrary, they have

139

divine power to demolish strongholds. We demolish arguments and every pretension that sets itself up against the knowledge of God, and we take captive every thought to make it obedient to Christ (2 Cor. 10:3-5).

Proper preparation and proper support are necessary for any battle. If you don't know scriptural answers for people's questions, study and ask others to find out. If you don't understand, for example, the New Age ideas you hear, ask questions and read articles and books on the subject.

If you are going to confront anti-Christian ideas and be involved with people who accept them, you must be upheld with much support. Stay involved in the regular study of the Bible on your own and in a Bible study group. Worship in church and alone. Seek out Christian fellowship even if you can't find a "perfect" church. Continue to pray with others and by yourself.

And remember who the enemy is. It isn't the people you're trying to witness to. Unless they are seriously committed to opposing God, they are not even the enemy's direct representatives. The enemy is Satan and the "powers of this dark world . . . the spiritual forces of evil in the heavenly realms" (Eph. 6:12).

If we take him on in our own strength, we'll be quickly defeated. But in Christ we will be victors. "You, dear children, are from God and have overcome them, because the one who is in you is greater than the one who is in the world" (1 John 4:4).

3. *We have to "butt in"—in love.* While we were working on this chapter, the *Christianity Today* article up for study in Dale's adult Sunday School class raised this very issue of how much responsibility we should take for lead-

ing each other onto the right road. George Brushaber writes, "I really don't want to be a busybody intruding into other people's lives. But I can't help believing that this is what is expected of me by the teaching of Scripture. To 'butt in' is biblical. Remembering that all those who are redeemed and following Christ are described as priests, I note what Malachi included in his description of the ideal priest of God (chap. 2): To worship, to give instruction in righteousness, and to 'turn many from sin.' It is the latter task that sometimes requires that I 'butt in' to somebody else's business" ("Minding Someone Else's Business," *Christianity Today*, September 16, 1988, p.11). Brushaber goes on to emphasize the love, humility, and wisdom we need as we carry out our responsibility to confront sin.

It's risky to enter into loving dialogue with people who are sold on false messages. Warfare is risky. Victories are won by taking chances. If you've prepared yourself and are taking advantage of a good support group and depending on the Holy Spirit, you can be sure of God's protection. You'll be under attack, tempted, and sometimes stung by others' words and actions, but you will be on the winning side.

Dialogue includes listening to what people are saying so you understand what they believe then persuasively explaining what you believe. Of course that includes explaining what you think is wrong with what they believe but in a way that shows you value the other person despite your disagreement. Listen for ideas which are inconsistent with each other and with reality. Look for evidence that those ideas are failing to produce the results people want. Show how Christ offers what people really want, deep down inside.

Why bother with all this? Because there is a tremendous need and because people matter to God. We live in a confused culture. People are desperately trying to fill inborn needs while shutting out God who made them. The result is chaotic thinking.

Our Needy World

How is America thinking in the late eighties? We have abandoned reason for faith in nonrational, subjective feelings. We are hungry for personal power, frightened of the future, and on the lookout for anything which promises success and gain. Through mistrust and ignorance we have divorced ourselves from historic values. We are individualistic to the point of being self-serving, amoral, self-centered, and materialistic; we accept contradictory "truths" as equally valid; we are spiritually malnourished.

Such a scenario doesn't have to cause despair. The world in which these false messages are running wild is also a world in which the Holy Spirit is alive and active. It is the world which God "so loved . . . that He gave His one and only Son, that whoever believes in Him shall not perish but have eternal life" (John 3:16).

A professor of psychology, apparently writing from a non-Christian perspective, offers an interesting explanation for the dramatic rise in depression in people 25 to 44 years old. He makes the case that this is the generation which saw the failure of traditional institutions and therefore now pins all its hopes on its own individuality. But we ourselves are not strong enough to provide the meaning, satisfaction, and purpose we expect and demand of them. So, staring into our mirrors, we fall into disappointed melancholy.

When people no longer believe that their country is powerful and benevolent, that the family can be a source of enduring unity and support *or that a relationship with God is important,* where else can they turn for identity, satisfaction and hope? Many people turn to a very small and frail unit indeed: the self. . . . In a self standing alone without the buffer of larger beliefs, helplessness and failure can all too easily become hopelessness and despair. . . . Surely one necessary (although hardly sufficient) condition for finding meaning in our lives is an attachment to something larger than the lonely self. *To the extent that young people now find it hard to take seriously their relationship with God,* to care about their relationship with the country or to be part of a large and abiding family, they will find it very difficult to find meaning in life. To put it another way, the self is a very poor site for finding meaning (Martin E.P. Seligman, "Boomer Blues," *Psychology Today,* October 1988, pp. 50–55; emphasis added).

Every day we are with people—or can be with them if we seek them out—who are leaning on their own individuality and finding it is too frail to hold them. Many of them are not as satisfied with their lives as they look on the outside. Frightening as it is to approach them, we can look for open doors and go through them when they open to us.

A Wise and Gentle Approach

Wearing the armor of God does not mean we clank up to people and brandish our swords. God's armor is the invisible armor of His spiritual protection. His sword is the Word, which works internally where our human arguments cannot go: "The word of God is living and active. Sharper than any double-edged sword, it penetrates even to dividing soul and spirit, joints and marrow; it judges the thoughts and attitudes of the heart" (Heb. 4:12). Our approach to friends, neighbors, and coworkers can be wise and gentle:

● "I'm interested in people's ideas about God. What do you think about Him?"

● "There's been a lot of controversy lately about who Jesus Christ was. Do you think we can know what Jesus actually did and taught?"

● "I didn't quite understand what you said the other day about all of us being part of God. Could you explain what you meant by that?"

● "Are you familiar with the Bible? Have you ever read it? What do you think of it? Would you be interested in studying some parts of it?"

The very evening we're completing this chapter, we'll be hosting a group of miscellaneous people for a Halloween party. We say *miscellaneous* because they are from all kinds of backgrounds, immersed in all kinds of beliefs. Some are married, some single. All are at different stages in their spiritual journeys. Paul reminded the Corinthians, who lived in an immoral pagan society, "I have written you in my letter not to associate with sexually immoral people—not at all meaning the people of this world who are immoral, or the greedy and swindlers, or idolators. In that case you would have to leave this world" (1 Cor. 5:9-10). We daily walk in two worlds, physically among unbelievers but spiritually with Christ. We must listen, know what we believe, and then pray we can butt in, with love.

"Remember this: Whoever turns a sinner away from his error will save him from death and cover many sins" (James 5:20). Among all the false messages that bombard us, may we and you and all of us, with God's help, be able to do exactly that.